ADELE RICKERBY

PROMISE
THE
I KEPT

**A MOTHER'S JOURNEY TO SAVE A CHILD FROM THE
POVERTY AND SQUALOR OF POST-COLD WAR ROMANIA**

2020 Revised edition

Mereo Books

Mereo Books 2nd Floor, 6-8 Dyer Street,
Cirencester, Gloucestershire, GL7 2PF

An imprint of Memoirs Book www.mereobooks.com and www.memoirsbooks.co.uk

The Promise I Kept: 978-1-909544-50-5

First published in Great Britain in 2013
by Mereo Books, an imprint of Memoirs Books.

Copyright ©2020

Adele Rickerby has asserted her right under the Copyright Designs and
Patents Act 1938 to be identified as the author of this work.

All of the events in this memoir are true to the best of the author's memory. Some names and identifying features have been changed in order to protect the identity of certain parties. Some events have been compressed and some dialogue has been recreated. The views expressed in this memoir are solely those of the author. The content is for informational purposes only and cannot be construed as professional advice.

Although the author and publisher have made every effort to ensure that the information in this book was correct at the time of going to press, we do not assume and hereby disclaim any liability to any party for any loss, damage or disruption caused by errors or omissions.

The address for Memoirs Books can be found at www.mereobooks.com

Mereo Books Ltd. Reg. No. 12157152

Typeset in 11/15pt Century Schoolbook by Wiltshire Associates.

Printed and bound in Great Britain

This is a very powerful book, meaningful, speaking straight to the soul, heart-touching. Vivid descriptions bring the reader at the core of events and situations. A lot of suffering that generated so much ambition, determination, so much courage in a person weakened and vulnerable due to so many trials and tribulations. Love and self-sacrifice coming from a broken heart.

A wounded soul has so much power and nothing can stop it when it has started on its way. A huge ambition compensates all the frustrations and by saving another soul you have saved yourself. A very good book, a thrilling read, a wonderful writer.

Teo Chariessa, Conop, Romania

ACKNOWLEDGEMENT

There are not enough words to thank Tom for his generously donated photographs. His iconic photos of Romania have brought life and soul to the 2020 revised version of my memoir, which is a little piece of my heart, and I am eternally grateful. Tom does not need words to tell a story. Each one of his images captures a moment in the lives of Romanians and speaks volumes. Words can easily be read and forgotten, but you cannot easily forget Tom's poignant and sometimes confronting images. They are a powerful portrait of the inhuman conditions and suffering of a lost generation of Romania's abandoned children.

Tom has also written a memoir about his life-changing journeys to Romania, where you will see more of his iconic photos.

"Even the Sparrow has Found a Home" by Thomas B. Szalay.

Our personal stories are a footnote to history.

ROMANIAN REMINISCENCES

by Thomas Szalay

It's been nearly three decades since an eleven-year-old boy helped me to discover a world I didn't know existed; the lives of Romanian orphans. I met Izidor Ruckel the day he landed at the airport in San Diego, California on assignment for the *Union-Tribune*, the city's newspaper. He travelled a long way from a hellish place that was commonly known as the Institute for the Unsalvageable in Sighetu Marmatiei to live with his new adoptive family, Danny and Marlys Ruckel and their three daughters. I was the outsider, a photojournalist eager to capture moments with my Nikon camera. The time I shared with Izidor and the Ruckel family has deepened my sense of connection, compassion and advocacy for those without a voice.

Travelling to northern Romania in 1992 was akin to walking into a time machine. When I witnessed peasants harvesting hay with an antiquated machine, I imagined that my Hungarian ancestors might have done the same thing. Local residents and Roma (gypsies) went about daily life in big cities and small villages. They spun yarn by hand, herded sheep and played cards. They smoked like chimneys and drank plenty of wine, vodka and Palinka to sand down life's hard edges. As an adult, Izidor became famous from his interviews on Romanian television, and the public consumed them like a baby nursing. He shared his struggles as an abandoned infant when he contracted polio from an infected syringe.

In 2015, I returned to Romania to work with Izidor. One evening, a woman was unloading some groceries as Izidor and I returned to our apartment. She recognised him and invited us up for a visit. She was a complete stranger, but she trusted Izidor and started to tell him about her life. He listened patiently, like a friend. The institution where Izidor grew up is no longer in use, but the rooms, filled with piles of clothes, stuffed animals, rusty beds, and broken toilets, cry silently.

Izidor and I talked about how this old concrete detritus of misery should become a memorial to the innocents who shared the haunted legacy of a distorted decree. This book tells Adele's story. My images hopefully will help you, the reader, understand why so many caring people chose to go to Romania and adopt. They were called by compassion to help abandoned children. Lessons learned in the Romania Orphan stories three decades ago remind us during this time of the Covid-19 pandemic, to act on building connections and community with a commitment to listen and be there for each other.

Thomas Szalay, June 2020

INTRODUCTION

I did not grow up in a Christian home. When Sunday came around, it was not a day for church but for a Sunday drive. We usually bought an ice-cream. Inevitably, I would get car-sick and vomit.

At age seventeen, when I left home to move into the nurses' home, there was a Baptist Church across the road and after an invitation from a lovely young Christian lady from Navigators, I started to attend. I asked Jesus into my life and was baptised. My faith has sustained me.

I journeyed to Romania armed with a Bible and my favourite Bible verses, one of which is Romans 8:28 New International Version (NIV):

'And we know that in all things, God works for the good of those who love him, who have been called according to his purposes'.

Instead of Sunday drives on Sundays, I took my children to church; mainstream Anglican and Baptist churches were where my daughters learnt Christian principles, based on sound Biblical teaching. Melannie attended a high-school youth group and volunteered at kids' church and Natasha attended the very popular Kid's Holiday Club.

I am inspired by the humble heroes, ordinary people, many

of whom are Christian, achieving extraordinary things and changing the destinies of Romania's abandoned children.

'Religion that God our Father accepts as pure and faultless is this; to look after orphans and widows in their distress and to keep oneself from being polluted by the world.' James 1:27 NIV

You will find posts about these people and the child welfare charities they have established or work for, on my website: www.thepromisekept.co, named after the title of my memoir. I also have a community Facebook page, thepromisekept.co, where you will find posts about the wonderful work of these organisations.

My favourite Psalm is Psalm 91:

1 Whoever dwells in the shelter of the Most High will rest in the shadow of the Almighty.
2 I will say of the LORD, "He is my refuge and my fortress, my God, in whom I trust."
3 Surely he will save you from the fowler's snare and from the deadly pestilence.
4 He will cover you with his feathers, and under his wings you will find refuge; his faithfulness will be your shield and rampart.
5 You will not fear the terror of night, nor the arrow that flies by day,
6 nor the pestilence that stalks in the darkness, nor the plague that destroys at midday.
7 A thousand may fall at your side, ten thousand at your right hand, but it will not come near you.
8 You will only observe with your eyes and see the punishment of the wicked.
9 If you say, "The LORD is my refuge" and you make the

Most High your dwelling,
10 no harm will overtake you, no disaster will come near your tent.
11 For he will command his angels concerning you to guard you in all your ways;
12 they will lift you up in their hands, so that you will not strike your foot against a stone.
13 You will tread on the lion and the cobra; you will trample the great lion and the serpent.
14 "Because he loves me," says the LORD, "I will rescue him; I will protect him, for he acknowledges my name.
15 He will call on me, and I will answer him; I will be with him in trouble, I will deliver him and honour him.
16 With long life I will satisfy him and show him my salvation."

CHAPTER ONE

Megan met me after school. "One, two, three, four, kick the teacher out the door," she sang loudly, and rather disrespectfully, I thought. She didn't possess any dress sense either, and wore a bright red woollen cardigan all buttoned up down the front and a yellow skirt, whereas I was all demure in my favourite faded floral skirt and a cream-coloured cardigan over a nondescript blouse. I liked that skirt because, when I sat down, it spread out in a circle all around me, like a tutu. Like all my clothes, the skirt was a hand-me-down.

Megan's red hair hung down over her freckled face. My long blond hair was tied back tightly, with a rubber band, into a ponytail. Not a breath of wind or a drop of rain touched our innocent childish cheeks as we walked home that still, sunny afternoon. We bent down to pick dandelions and blew gently, lips puckered, onto their rounded heads. We watched, enchanted, as their delicate tendrils danced for us in the air. I was careful to keep out of the gutter, as it wasn't true that I was a guttersnipe.

"Sticks and stones will break my bones but names will never hurt me," I chanted defiantly to the ever-attentive Megan.

We walked past the old wooden homestead with the huge macrocarpas hedge along the front and a hole in the middle of the hedge for a white, wooden gate to go. My newly-married uncle resided in that house; we couldn't go to his wedding because we were too poor to purchase the new clothes we needed to wear.

Megan and I crossed the road and stayed comfortably close to each other as we walked past the house where the witch lived. The house was all dark and dingy with black blinds over the windows and the garden overgrown. It was just the kind of house where you believed a witch would live.

"We'd better hurry before she comes out and puts a bad spell on us," I told Megan as we ran past the house.

Not far to go now before we are both safely home. Around the corner and up the hill. I couldn't wait to take off my bandages. I suffered badly with atopic eczema. My mother's solution to this problem was to send me off to school with my long, thin arms covered in bandages she had made by tearing old, white cotton sheets into strips. The thick, gooey ointment underneath the bandages was to stop the itch and promote healing.

At the top of a steep hill ending in a cul-de-sac, I would stop to catch my breath and look at the magical view whilst Megan ran on ahead. I could see the houses, gardens, trees and hills that I loved and which were so much a part of my childhood. In the distance was the steep hill with the narrow sheep track ringed around it. The sheep walked slowly, in single file, from right to left, with heads bowed, along the narrow track. Other hills looked almost as if they had been dabbed with bright yellow paint, because the gorse bushes were in full bloom.

I walked down the lane to my home. It was very quiet. I was the first of seven children to arrive home that day. Like so many other mothers who work hard to keep the home fires burning, there was nothing remarkable about mine, other than the fact that she gave birth to seven children. My mother had thick, wavy, brown hair, soft, clear skin and a broad, engaging smile. Her beautiful blue eyes were a problem to her because she was totally colour blind, shortsighted and susceptible to glare. She could not see to thread a needle or drive a car, and was totally housebound. In keeping with her nature, she suffered these disabilities without complaint.

At first, I couldn't find her. She wasn't in any of her usual places. She wasn't downstairs bending over the washing machine; she wasn't hanging clothes on the line in the backyard. She wasn't in the kitchen, or on the telephone. I finally found her lying on the couch in the lounge. She was very still and her eyes were closed.

My innocent childhood died that day, and thirteen weeks later, so did my mother.

She went into hospital to have her gallstones removed. The story goes that when the doctors opened her up, they found that she was riddled with bowel cancer. There was nothing they could do except remove the gallstones, stitch her back up and send her home. They gave her thirteen weeks to live and she died thirteen weeks later to the day. She was forty-two. I was twelve and a half.

My father chose not to tell me, Alena or Kent, the three youngest children as we were known, that our mother was dying, believing it was in our best interests. It must have been a burden for our four older siblings not to tell us.

Mum came home from hospital and we moved to the corner store, with house attached, that my parents had bought before my mother became ill. They had planned to start a new life managing this business together. My Aunty Ina, who had got married late in life to my mother's brother, Uncle George, was a trained nurse. She provided palliative care to our mother at our new home. Aunty Ina's tender loving care enabled my mother to stay at home surrounded by her family until just a few days before the end. I could see that my mother was sick, having lost so much weight, and now being very weak. But the concept of dying was foreign to my childish brain and never entered my head. Mum spent her last few days in hospital, but I was not taken to see her. I did not get to say goodbye. Not even in that childish way of saying goodbye with the excited expectation of seeing her whole and home again.

This was in the days before Elizabeth Kubler Ross' ground-breaking book *On Death and Dying* (1969), which first discussed the five stages of grief which she had identified.

Until then, death was separated from life to the extent that it was never talked about, not even with the dying person.

The shop with the living quarters attached was on a corner. There was a big upstairs lounge with beautiful bay windows. From there you could sit on the cushioned window seat and look out across the suburbs to the still calm of the harbour. I could see, but not hear, seagulls circling below threatening dark clouds. It was a cold wintry day in August and we were expecting more rain.

Winter was appalling. My father called us all up to the lounge and broke the harrowing news of our mother's death. I felt her spirit protectively close to me and I cried out to her from deep within my very being to return to us. But it was too late. She was gone, her life extinguished.

As an adult, I journeyed to a quiet, still place in my heart where I was able to say goodbye to my mother, confident that she heard me. A place in my heart strewn with delicate, fragrant rose petals is a memorial to her.

CHAPTER TWO

My father was a tall, thin man who went bald at a very early age. He was always of neat, clean and tidy appearance, clean and polished shoes included. He became highly respected in the community for building up a successful business and for looking after seven children on his own after his wife died. During the eight years that he owned the business, several other corner stores in the vicinity closed down, but my father's continued to thrive.

    My four older siblings, two brothers and two sisters, drifted away with boyfriends, girlfriends, part-time jobs and university studies. So from the age of twelve and a half to the time I was seventeen, it was increasingly left up to me and my younger sister, Alena, to take on the role of parenting Kent, our youngest brother, who was only five when our mother died. We also had to do the domestics and help in the shop. This was all unpaid. Working in the shop included serving customers, dusting shelves, unpacking and pricing stock and putting it on the shelves and cleaning the fridges and pie ovens. There wasn't much time left to complete homework and study for exams.

We had a roster system in place for domestic duties. They included cooking, setting the table and washing and drying the dishes. My eldest brother did the family washing and I tackled the ironing. My cooking was very basic. One of the first meals I ever cooked was mashed potatoes, peas and curried sausages. My father always appreciated anything my sister and I cooked. There were never any complaints.

I started menstruating when I was thirteen and experienced painful, heavy bleeding. In the same way that there was an unwritten rule that you never discussed death, there was also an unwritten rule that you never discussed menstruation. I had never heard the word "endometriosis", so I did not know until many years later that I had it. There was no such thing as the Endometriosis Association. I would walk home from school wearing two sanitary napkins to contain the blood flow and run myself a hot bath.

Soaking in that bath in seclusion and silence was heaven. It was a big, deep bath facing a window and there always seemed to be plenty of hot water. When the water went lukewarm, I would just top it up with more hot water. I would sit there watching the dark red blood flow freely from the innermost cavity of my womb, out between my long, skinny legs and into the hot, still water. Sometimes the pain and the bleeding were so bad that I could not even go to school.

Eventually I took a bus to see my family GP and he prescribed the pill, but by the time I was seventeen years old, I had had my first operation, a dilation and curettage of my uterus, or D&C as it was more commonly known. I was afraid that people thought I was having an abortion.

Soon after, I moved to the nurses' home with one small suitcase carrying all my possessions and started work as a nurse's aid. I had to do this for six months until I was old enough to start my nursing training. Career choices for women were limited in those days to nursing, teaching or receptionist work.

A highlight of my three-and-a-half year general nursing training was the six months I spent at the Queen Mary Maternity Hospital. I loved working with the new mums and babies in the post-natal ward. It was a very happy place to be, full of new life and health instead of despair and disease. On my days off, I would catch the bus home to help in the shop or clean the kitchen.

Tony was late for our first date. It was a blind date for the Dine & Dance my nursing class was having in November of 1977 to celebrate our graduation. He had already graduated from university with a Masters degree in Geology and I found him interesting. Our relationship took the usual route of living together, trips overseas, engagement, and eventually marriage. But I had serious doubts along the road and called the engagement off. Tony talked me round and the marriage went ahead.

Shortly after, we were staying with Tony's family and it was not going well. I left and went to stay with my father. I had only been there one night and was still in bed the next morning when my father came in and said angrily and accusingly, "You've had a good run out of me girl, now get up and get out of here!"

I had no money, no job and nowhere else to go, so I had no choice but to go back to the marriage. Tony got a job in Australia, so we came here for the mining boom. We were based in Brisbane and a year went by quickly, but I hardly saw him as he was away for up to six weeks at a time on exploration geology trips in Central Queensland. I made a life for myself. I got a job as a doctor's receptionist and I had frequent visitors from New Zealand to keep me company.

I was committed to my marriage and lived in the hope that my husband would change. I wanted to have children, but my husband's long and frequent absences made this difficult. So he got a job as a geologist in a small country town, where he said we would only stay for two years. We lived in ex-housing commission houses purchased by the mining company to accommodate their employees. Rent was a token $8 per week, to entice workers to come and work in the harsh, hot climate of the isolated country town.

After dinner one evening, my friend Emily and I removed ourselves from the dining room and made our way into the kitchen, as I wanted to make coffee. Emily, never one to mince words and sounding somewhat perturbed said, "He looks nothing like I thought your husband would, Adele. I thought he would be taller. At least taller than you. And his hair. Where did he get those curls from? Where did you get him from, Adele?"

"Should I take him back to where I got him from?" I asked Emily. The ensuing laughter broke the tension between us. It was too late for that, I thought. Good Christian wives do not leave their husbands under any circumstances.

"He loves to talk about his work, doesn't he," Emily said. What she really meant was that the entire conversation over dinner had been about his work at the mine. "Where has he been anyway?" was Emily's next question. "Out gold panning," I replied.

On Tuesday evenings Tony played squash. On Fridays they all got off work early to play golf. On other evenings he played tennis and indoor cricket.

CHAPTER THREE

"I want to go home," I said to Margaret.

"You should wait until the doctor comes to see you before you discharge yourself," she replied.

Margaret, mature fifties, grey hair permed close to her head, was sitting on the bed opposite mine. She wore the mandatory hospital garb; nightgown, dressing gown and slippers. I was not happy with this situation at all. The evening before, I had driven the short distance from our mine-owned ex-housing commission house to the Biloela Country Hospital. I parked the car. Then I went inside to be admitted. Old white paint on old wooden walls. Big verandas all around. Tin roof. Drab interior.

A girlfriend had recently given birth here. Badly deformed, the baby died hours later. There were clusters of babies being born with hair-lips, cleft palates and heart defects. This was cotton-growing country. For over 20 years the farmers used poisonous sprays on the cotton. Some mornings I would wake up to the sound of the crop dusters.

Looking up, I would see them spraying and smell the chemicals. I was horrified.

I rang the Department of Primary Industries. They were obliging. I was told that the majority of spraying was done over the summer months. Amongst other chemicals the farmers used Agent Orange, the same chemicals used by the Americans during the Vietnam War, to spray over the cotton to defoliate it prior to harvesting.

I had just arrived from nuclear-free New Zealand. The chemicals the farmers were using in Biloela had long been banned there. New research had shown a clear correlation between the use of these chemicals and birth defects. Another girlfriend had a baby in Biloela. That baby died too. I decided that if I was to get pregnant I would not live in Biloela during the first three crucial months of my pregnancy.

"How's the knitting circle going?" My GP asked me when I went to him for a consultation. He was referring to the close-knit circle of mine employees' wives, of which I was one. When I talked to him about the spraying and birth defects, he replied, "The green skin on potatoes is poisonous too."

Earlier that morning the same GP had performed a surgical procedure, a D&C. 'Thank you for your concern, Margaret," I replied. "But I really want to go home."

My GP could take ages, I thought. I was tired and very hungry after being subject to nil by mouth since midnight. Also, I didn't want to stay and discuss my personal medical details with Margaret, well-meaning as she was. Her husband, Jim, was on the mine staff as well. There was no privacy. On several occasions my girlfriends knew my business before I did.

"Jim says he hasn't seen Tony at work recently," Margaret said, hoping for information. Occasionally Tony would travel to conferences.

"He's gone over to Perth for the America's Cup," I replied. "He's a keen sailor. He used to sail a catamaran in New Zealand."

I got dressed and, leaving Margaret with a worried look on her face, drove the short distance home. I boiled myself an egg, had a slice of toast and a cup of tea and went to bed to sleep off the effects of the anaesthetic undisturbed. I didn't suffer any side effects from the surgery, nor did I gain any benefit. It soon proved to be a complete waste of time. That particular operation did not alleviate my endometriosis at all. So it wasn't long before I drove myself down to Brisbane to see an obstetrician and gynaecologist who had been highly recommended to me, Dr Peter Monks.

After examining me, Dr Monks said I needed more surgery. This would be my third operation. He found that my pelvic cavity and uterus were full of endometrial growths and that my fallopian tubes had collapsed under the weight of them and my uterus was completely retroverted. Dr Monks was an excellent surgeon. He removed the growths and repaired the damage. Fortunately my fallopian tubes were not blocked or damaged. I returned home to recover, and to both Dr Monks' and my astonishment, I conceived five months later. This felt like a miracle.

Because of my medical history, I did not want to risk giving birth in the small country town hospital. Fortunately for me, my eldest sister and her husband had recently moved from New Zealand to Brisbane, so I went to stay with them one month before my baby was delivered. I had an emergency caesarean section and delivered a beautiful, healthy baby girl whom I called Melannie. That was my fourth operation.

After Melannie and I had been in the maternity hospital for nearly a week, it was time to go home. I booked a taxi to take us from the hospital to the domestic airport. When we arrived at the terminal, I was dismayed to find it crowded with passengers. In fact, I had never seen the terminal so crowded. It was because of a bad electrical storm; all flights had been delayed by at least half an hour. I was not happy at the prospect of waiting in a crowded terminal with a newborn baby and a sore stomach from a caesarean. I hated flying and often got sick.

As I was standing there surveying the situation, my husband's boss, Warren, came over to me. Most fortunately for me, Warren was on the same flight home as Melannie and me. He had been in Brisbane for business. I was so relieved to see him and felt that he was heaven sent. Warren booked a seat next to Melannie and me, and once the storm had passed, we finally boarded our flight home. Melannie, barely one week old, was having her first plane trip. Fortunately she travelled well, I didn't get sick and Warren was there to help me.

The plane trip was not lengthy, only 600 kms. My husband met us at the tiny rural airport, and we drove home. I was finally back in my own home with my baby, having been away for five weeks.

One December night not long after our return home, I fed Melannie and put her down to sleep. Although we had air conditioning it was still very hot. I was breastfeeding her and I was tired. I went to bed myself, and as I laid my head on the pillow, I started to cry. My husband responded by immediately getting very angry. With both his legs, he kicked me out of the bed and onto the floor. I lay motionless, dazed and shocked on the floor beside our double bed. Something had torn deep within my heart, the very core of my being. I could not move.

Tony lay on his side of the bed, silent, his back turned towards me. It had been only weeks since I had flown back from Brisbane with Melannie. I did not have any family to support me. It was some time before I was able to crawl back into bed and get some sleep.

In the morning I got up and carried on; I had a baby to look after. Like so many other women isolated in a country not their own, I was physically and financially dependent on my husband.

When Melannie was eight months old, the endometriosis returned with a vengeance. I had read that pregnancy and breastfeeding help to keep the disease under control, but not in my case. Once again I was experiencing a lot of pain and heavy bleeding, making me tired and anaemic. Medication helped to a certain extent, but it had very strong side effects, and I could not take it indefinitely. My husband told me that there was nothing wrong with me, that it was all in my head.

Eventually I took Melannie and drove back to Brisbane to see Dr Monks. Before I had Melannie, I would drive the 600 kms to Brisbane in one day, but I could not expect her to cope with this, so I would drive half the distance with her, stopping regularly on the way. There were some great country town bakeries. By the afternoon we would be halfway, so we would stop at a motel and resume our journey in the morning. Melannie travelled well, and there was lots for her to look at along the way.

In Brisbane I saw Dr Monks. He wanted to operate on me straight away, but I drove back home with Melannie and spent a week getting ready and cajoling my husband into supporting me. We returned to Brisbane. I had a hysterectomy and an ovary removed while Tony looked after Melannie. She was three years old. It was my fifth operation.

Once we returned home, I insisted that after seven long years of living in an isolated country town, it was time we moved. I sent my husband's resumes off to mining companies and he got a job in Cairns. That was like going from one extreme to the other – from a hot, dry, dusty isolated country town to subtropical Queensland.

Melannie and I settled into life in Cairns and made new friends. We had a quarter-acre section with a swimming pool which was used a lot by our neighbours' children. My husband and I started renovating the old house we had bought and landscaping the garden, which was a fertile, overgrown subtropical rainforest. The block of land sloped down to a delightful creek, with water running over slippery smooth rocks. My barren body was healing from my fifth operation, but the mother in me would not be silenced. She talked to me every day and told me that she wanted another child. It was as if a seed of hope which refused to die had been divinely planted within my barren body.

In spite of the difficult circumstances of my relationship, I wanted another baby; a girl, a sister for Melannie. So I embarked upon the arduous process of applying through the Department of Family Services, who fortunately at the time still had a regional office in Cairns, to be approved for intercountry adoption.

After three years and extensive paperwork, we were finally approved to adopt a little girl from Thailand. I bought Melannie, now six years old, a brown doll, and prepared her little heart for a sister as best I could.

I made direct enquiries to the social worker at the orphanage in Thailand, something which was not allowed by the Department of Family Services. I learned that because we already had a child, my file was not a priority. Priority was given to childless couples, and there were 300 of them on the waiting list before me. The social worker told me I would be waiting at least another three years.

My disappointment was palpable. But this was how the Department of Family Services operated. They withheld important information or simply did not tell the truth, so that prospective adoptive couples were kept in the dark and unable to make wise and well-informed decisions.

At this time news reports were coming out of Romania of the 100,000 children abandoned in orphanages there. I wrote to Gerry Hand, the then Minister for Immigration, enquiring if Australians could adopt from Romania. My husband and I had become Australian citizens. Soon after, the Minister's reply came back. In his letter, Gerry Hand stated that all these children would be reunited with their families when the economic situation improved. The governments of England, America, Canada, Ireland and New Zealand and other countries around the world did not share this view, and were assisting couples with the necessary legal requirements in order for them to adopt abandoned children from Romania legally.

Estimates are that around ten thousand children from institutions were adopted internationally from Romania between 1990 and 2001. In 2004, following new laws, international adoptions became virtually impossible.

Statistics from Taylor and Francis online Adoption Quarterly. Historical Perspectives and Recent Statistics, Volume 23, 2020

You wake up one morning to the sound of history knocking loudly, impatiently, persistently, at your door. To answer it is to take a leap of faith into your future.

In a chance phone call from an acquaintance in Brisbane,

she informed me that she knew of a couple, Narelle and Stephen Walker, living in Brisbane, who had recently returned from Romania via New Zealand, having adopted a baby boy and a baby girl.

Narelle, being aware of the Australian government's long-standing bias against inter-country adoption, went to the media to promote awareness and the knowledge that New Zealand citizens living in Australia could legally adopt from Romania through the New Zealand government.

Needless to say, I immediately made contact with Narelle and started the application process to adopt from Romania as a New Zealand citizen. My adopted child would automatically have New Zealand citizenship by descent.

I was most fortunate in that Alena, my youngest sister, was living in Wellington, the capital of New Zealand, with her husband Russell and their three young daughters. I sent all my documents to Alena, who took them to the Department of Internal Affairs, the Department of External Affairs and to be witnessed and signed by a Notary Public. In the meantime, I packed my bags and booked my tickets.

My mother-in-law was coming to Australia for a wedding, so she came up to Cairns to look after Melannie. My husband stayed in Cairns on the pretext that he needed to work and to look after Melannie.

There was an anxious 24-hour period when my documents went missing in the mail after Alena posted them back to Australia. I located them and they arrived just hours before I was due to leave.

CHAPTER FOUR

A tiny, dark, dismal hotel room on a drizzly morning in Tokyo. I was alone to face my fear, which was like a black wall of dark rock threatening to fall in upon me, to weigh me down so I could neither go forward into the unknown future nor backwards into the safe security of my past.

I was hungry and sick. I vomited. Empty and exhausted, I had to keep the wall from crashing in upon me. Fortunately, my flight did not leave until the afternoon. I had time to take control of my emotions, to calm and compose myself, to rest and to eat a little.

My first thoughts were of ringing my husband to come and rescue me, but I had come too far already. The pain and suffering I had experienced over so many years would amount to nothing, serve no purpose, if I were to turn back now. Something good and worthwhile had to be borne out of my infertility.

I made it onto my flight to Frankfurt. The hours were restful, uneventful. It was late afternoon when I arrived at Frankfurt airport. Ill-prepared for this journey, I made my first blunder. Circling the terminal in search of information that Easter holiday weekend, I found I could not book a ticket on Tarom Airlines, the cheap Romanian airline which would take me to Bucharest, only a journey of two hours, and I did not want to spend the money I had on an airfare.

Intuitively, I felt a great sense of urgency. I did not want to waste time and money staying in Frankfurt over the long Easter weekend, then catching a flight out on Tarom. I decided instead to go by train. I bought the ticket at the airport, booked a hotel room for the night and left by train the next morning. I had travelled by train before from Mexico City to the American border at Mexicali, and set out in a positive frame of mind, preferring going by train to flying.

The journey through Germany was clean, interesting and civilised; there was a buffet car and clean toilets. Occasionally I exchanged a few words in English with fellow passengers.

We changed trains in Vienna, which was a retrograde step into the filth and grime of a less affluent era. I shared my compartment with an elderly gentleman who sliced salami with a pocket-knife, placed it on dry bread and washed this humble repast down with a swig of whisky from a large bottle in a brown paper bag. He tried to warn me in broken English of impending trouble, stabbing at the air with his knife for effect.

Then the train stopped and eight Hungarian soldiers dressed in khaki uniforms, revolvers exposed on their hips, rushed onto the train and ran through the carriages, bearing down on us threateningly. "Passports!" they yelled in loud voices. I reluctantly handed over my passport to a tall soldier with a pock-marked face. He cried out in triumph to the other soldiers "NZ passport!" and waved it high above his head for all to see.

An official boarded the train and ordered me off. I argued back, refusing to leave the train. I said I had paid to go to Romania and stood my ground. He threw my two suitcases and sleeping bag out of the open carriage window and onto the railway track below. I had no choice but to take my briefcase with all my documents and get off the train. By this time, all the passengers were out of their seats, leaning out of the open carriage windows and surveying this spectacle. As I stood on an adjoining railway track surrounded by my luggage, the train, pitiless, left without me.

I gathered my belongings and walked towards a very old, small, wooden building, dark inside, white outside, from which officials were coming and going. The eight Hungarian soldiers were standing in a group off to my right, looking at me, watching and waiting.

After what seemed like hours, a middle-aged, well-dressed gentleman came striding towards me. He spoke English. He was the local taxi driver. He said this had happened before. The problem was, I did not have a visa.

I could not believe it. I was only transiting their country for a few hours en route to Romania. He said he could help. The train would arrive in Budapest at 8 pm, stop for an hour, and leave again at 9 pm. The taxi driver promised that he could have me in Budapest in time to catch the train before it left.

I had no choice but to trust this stranger. He had my passport. We bundled my belongings into the boot of his taxi and took off to get my visa. As I paid for it, using some cash I had in a canvas pouch hanging around my neck, it was impossible to hide the fact that I had additional money on me.

He then asked me for the equivalent of half a year's salary

to drive me across Hungary. The amount felt like an unspoken compromise of sorts. I duly paid. It was fortunate that I had a spare photo of myself for the visa.

Once back in the car, we detoured hastily through the deserted back streets of a small country town en route to a petrol station. I felt very vulnerable. I was a female foreigner alone in a car with a man who could rape me, steal the rest of my money and leave me for dead in the bushes on the roadside. No one would have known.

As we drove onto the highway, my fears subsided. I was simply on my way to Budapest with a middle-aged taxi driver who was married with children and had lived in the same village for eight years. But in the fading light, the scenery became oppressive; a barren landscape studded with concrete block apartment boxes.

At 8.45 pm, with only 15 minutes to spare, we arrived at the station in Budapest and found my train. We hurriedly unloaded my luggage from his boot and into the first empty carriage we saw. The taxi driver kissed my hand and thanked me profusely. I thanked him and said goodbye.

I resumed my journey through the relentless, cold night, but it seemed as if we were stopping every ten minutes. Each time I felt sick with apprehension as officials boarded the train, checked and stamped my passport and invaded the privacy of my personal belongings. Thank God I had a visa for Romania, I thought.

Icy whispers emerged from the snow as cold hands clutched at door handles. My compartment door handle was next. I didn't like the look of the two burly peasants rugged up in sheepskin jackets as they headed towards my compartment. I took a safety pin and used it to draw closed the curtains over my compartment door and window. This afforded me some privacy and deterred a few would-be intruders. The men would move the carriage door handle down and then try to push open the carriage door. Fortunately, the safety pin held the curtains firmly in place, and this prevented the door from opening.

Eventually we stopped stopping and I slept fitfully, thankful for the warmth and comfort of my sleeping bag.

Suddenly, jerked back into harsh reality by the train's brakes, I saw, illuminated through the evil black of the winter night by bare bulbs, several soldiers, bayoneted rifles at the ready, on guard. We were at a remote railway station. Again I felt threatened and vulnerable. Again I wished I was travelling with a male companion. Again I wished I could speak more than one language.

Finally free of the oppressive darkness, we travelled to meet the morning. Through a heavy pall of pollution I saw snow receding, revealing winter-barren earth. Everything was covered in grime and there was an unpleasant smell of urine. Stale urine stained the so-called toilet and surrounding floor. It was filthy.

Human beings, coal miners, were herded like cattle into the two-tiered train on the track beside me. At 7.15 am and nearing Bucharest, my train became a commuter train. I gathered my belongings, tidied myself up as best I could, unpinned the curtain and allowed four tidily dressed men, pressed for a place to sit, to share my compartment.

I was an unexpected oddity. We introduced ourselves. They spoke a little English. They were engineers who worked for the railway, on their way to a meeting in Bucharest. I explained my presence on the train. One young man told me, "Our country is poor, but our hearts are rich".

I had just travelled 1,480 kilometres by train and taxi

through Germany, Austria, Hungary and into Romania as far as the capital, Bucharest.

At the Gara De Nord Railway Station, I went into the Tourist Information Office to look for Michaela, who worked there. She had already looked after many adoptive parents and their babies in Bucharest, Narelle and her husband included. Narelle recommended that I stay with Michaela. I didn't have any other contacts. I looked at the staff. None of their badges held the name I was looking for.

After a couple of attempts, I found a young woman who spoke English. 'I want to see Michaela', I said to her. 'That's not possible', she replied. 'Michaela is on holidays for two weeks'. For a moment, I could not speak. Then they phoned her home. Thankfully, she was still in Bucharest.

While waiting for her to arrive, I was approached by a young male entrepreneur who offered me absolutely everything, including the kind of things it wasn't in my nature to purchase. I was hungry and thirsty, tired and desperate for a hot shower and to change into clean clothes. I stood silently and waited for what seemed like hours.

Finally, Michaela walked towards me. She was a big lady and I was soon to learn that she possessed an even bigger heart. Her friendly face beamed a reassuring smile as she stretched out her enormous arms towards me and welcomed me with an embrace.

Michaela was not alone. Accompanying her on this mission to rescue me was a much younger woman, Janet. She wore a warm winter coat and trousers over her voluptuous curves and her long mane of blonde bombshell hair fell down the back of her coat. Clean and fresh, Janet stood out from the crowd, contrasting against everyone and everything else, which appeared dirty, old and grimy.

Her pleasant voice and smile welcomed me quietly and hinted at curiosity. There were lots of questions about me she wanted answered.

That first meeting left an indelible impression on me. Fate had conspired to bring us together, same time, same place, but halfway around the world. Janet and her husband had already been in Bucharest, staying with Michaela, for six weeks, whilst processing their adoptions, a baby boy and a baby girl. Not knowing how much longer they would have to wait for home studies by overworked social workers, and for court dates, challenged their patience, but they possessed an iron will to succeed. Janet said she felt as if the rest of the world had forgotten them.

Michaela's home, luxurious by Romanian standards, was a haven of warmth, comfort, security and food, shared with English-speaking people. Michaela said I looked fragile. What did she mean, I wondered - physically or emotionally? I put the question aside in my mind, unanswered. There were too many other things to think about.

CHAPTER FIVE

Michaela, a woman of the Romanian Orthodox Church, said she believed we had been sent by God to adopt her country's children. The government's drive to increase Romania's population had led to the birth of thousands of unwanted babies. The human cost of this and the full horror of the government policy only came to light after the 1989 revolution, when the veil of secrecy was swept aside. It is estimated that there were 600-700 institutions in Romania housing approximately 100,000 abandoned children.

Women suffered especially under the rule of Ceausescu, because of the role they were forced to play in the government's population policy.

I now had to gather information, have my documents translated and make a decision as to how I was going to proceed with the adoption. My hostess, whose judgement I trusted, arranged an interview with a doctor. She spoke to him briefly, then handed the phone to me. We talked. I liked the sound of his voice. He said he knew of two babies, both abandoned in an orphanage, who were available for adoption. One was a boy; he wasn't sure whether the other was a boy or a girl. The doctor said he would ring me back the following afternoon. I said, "I look forward to meeting you." Gabriel replied, "I hope you are not disappointed."

The doctor did call around in the evening after phoning to say he was coming. When we met, I liked him instantly. I was far from disappointed in what I saw, despite his gaunt appearance and constant smoking. We talked at the dining room table, the focal point for all that was happening, while other couples and Michaela looked on and listened. This initial meeting was crucial. I understood the importance of it. I needed him to like me, to want to help me.

As we talked, there were many misunderstandings due to language and cultural differences. I pressed for clarification, but he was evasive. I touched his hand to emphasise my position. My time and funds were limited. I had only allowed four weeks, including the time I needed to spend in Wellington, New Zealand, finalising the adoption. I had a six-year-old daughter to return to.

He was very angry. "This is an adoption, not a shopping trip to the supermarket!" he said. I was very offended. "I did not intend shopping for babies as if I was at a supermarket," I told him.

We established a rapport. It seemed that the other baby available for adoption was a little girl after all, three and a half months old and in an orphanage. She had been there since she was one week old. I felt incredibly lucky. Everyone had been saying how difficult it was becoming to find a baby girl. Already I felt she was mine, and I was meant to have her.

While I was nursing, our time on the wards was interspersed with blocks of study, assignments, practical and theoretical exams. It was during one of these study blocks that a tutor, to whom I will be forever grateful, introduced the class to the theory John Bowlby had put forward in 1951 of maternal deprivation. Namely, it stated that the "prolonged deprivation of the young child of maternal care may have grave and far-reaching effects". John Bowlby was a British psychoanalyst and child psychiatrist. He wrote his theory about maternal deprivation in a report commissioned by the World Health Organisation titled 'Maternal Care and Mental Health'.

Knowledge is a powerful tool. With it we are able to make wise and well-informed decisions. Armed with Bowlby's theory of maternal deprivation and a mother's natural instinct, I decided I wanted a baby under six months of age. The general rule is that for every month an abandoned child is left in an institution it is developmentally delayed by two or three months. Studies of Romania's abandoned children reveal how damaging institutionalized care is. According to Dr. Victor Groza, PhD, LISW-S Grace F. Brody Professor of Parent-Child Studies, Director- Child Welfare Fellows Program, Jack, Joseph and Morton Mandel School of Applied Social Sciences, Case Western Reserve University, Cleveland, Ohio, "Institutionalized care causes problems with developmental, physical, psychological, social and brain health". Please see http://www.thepremisekept.co", Romania's Institutions for Abandoned Children Caused Life-Long Damage.

I gave Dr Gabriel power of attorney. I felt his superiority keenly, and this made me feel uncomfortable and inferior around him. I had completed my nursing degree in an era when doctors were looked up to as gods. You never questioned them and followed instructions implicitly. He was fluent in several languages, including English, and had been one of the top students in his class the year he graduated from medical school in Bucharest. It was wonderful, while living in a foreign country, to be able to converse with another adult in English.

He was attracted to younger women wearing mini-skirts, high heels, stockings, lots of makeup and jewellery and looking like they had just stepped out of the hairdressers, but I had nothing to boast about by way of looks. I am tall and slim with long blond hair tied back off my face. My blue eyes are set in a rather angular face and the only makeup I wear is lipstick. I have never worn expensive clothes, shoes, perfumes, jewellery or hairdos. My limited budget would never have covered such luxuries and they were never a priority in my life.

It was illegal for foreigners to enter orphanages or hospitals, but Gabriel had a special relationship with the director of the orphanage. Through her, he would arrange for the baby to be taken back home, hopefully by the weekend, when I would be able to see her. I would not be able to take custody of her until the custody papers had been signed at court and I had negative results from AIDs and Hepatitis B tests.

The baby's mother was young, about 20, and single. She hoped to get married, but the man she wanted to marry was not this child's father. He had abandoned them. He was a silent partner, an unknown identity. He had played his part in this drama, but now it seemed he didn't exist. He had left the stage.

There wasn't enough room for me at Michaela's house, which was already overcrowded. There were only three bedrooms and 10 people and more on the way.

CHAPTER SIX

I took a taxi to the bank, but my money had not yet arrived. So much effort to then have to turn around and go home empty-handed.

Naturally I didn't have a clue where I was. The young taxi driver who took me to the bank went out of his way and took me down a one-way street the wrong way to make it easier for me. Unfortunately he got caught and pulled over by a traffic official. I felt very sorry for him. He was probably going to be fined more than my taxi fare. Catching on quickly, I tried to bribe the official with a packet of cigarettes, but he waved me away, and I left the young taxi driver to meet his fate.

The bank for Foreign Exchange was a shock. No orderly queues, no computers, totally archaic and uncivilised. One first had to figure out how the system worked, which teller to go to for which transaction and at which time. It all took hours and there was lots of pushing and shoving, standing on people's toes, gesticulating, and huge sums of cash being counted out, stuffed into briefcases and carried away.

On the way home, the taxi driver got lost. They do not have road maps, but when they are uncertain they stop the taxi, hop out and ask another taxi driver for directions. The fare is only the equivalent of a dollar. Locals prefer to be paid in American currency.

While I was away, Michaela and her husband Mario made up Michaela's bed for me in her room. It was awkward. I said I couldn't have her sleeping in the shed out at the back of the yard. She was offended and thought I didn't like it there, but I needed to be with other people. I needed the security they gave. I could not face being alone and isolated by myself in a hotel room. The matter rested for the time being. I could do nothing but humbly accept her hospitality. To keep busy I vacuumed, dusted, and washed floors.

Michaela's room was a haven. It was like a boudoir. I had it all to myself, but it was not totally private. One door led to the only bathroom and toilet and Michaela and Mario needed to use this for access to their clothes in the wardrobes. The other double glass door led into another bedroom. On the opposite wall was a window opening onto the backyard. Below this was a heater. Great for drying my clothes, which I washed by hand. But the air was so polluted that garments hanging on the clothes line dried grimy and there weren't enough pegs or line for everyone to use. A large framed picture of a bare-breasted woman, naked and in repose, adorned one wall. The pallor of her skin contrasted against the dark of the ill-lit room. The furniture was solid and basic.

That night I dreamed of donkeys and daffodils and kind-hearted Mario ploughing the fields. The feelings of peace my dream engendered were in contrast to those I had experienced most over the years, so I luxuriated in their warmth, not wanting to let them go, to face the harsh realities of my life.

Sadly Michaela did not have any biological children, but she treated all the adopted children as her own. They were on temporary loan to her during the agonising wait to finalise their adoptions. Michaela was a big woman with an even bigger heart. With plenty of room in it for all the babies and their adoptive parents who came into her fold. No doubt Mumma Michaela had her favourites amongst them, but she treated all equally, never showing any favouritism.

For many an hour Michaela would sit in her position at the end of the dining room table, her massive arms embracing two babies at once. Her curvaceous bosom flowed out over the top of the deep purple dressing gown she wore constantly, barely covering her up.

The next day was a day to remember. The doctor arrived at 8.30 am, just as I was getting out of bed. I hadn't been expecting him and wasn't ready, and he was annoyed. Michaela made us eat an omelette and I had a quick shower before the driver arrived.

We sped through Bucharest, dodging the massive potholes and heading out past a huge oil refinery belching forth fire and heavy liquid black smoke from its chimneys. We passed many broken-down cars whose owners either couldn't afford to fix them or couldn't get parts. We had to queue for petrol and people lined up to buy bread.

It took about two hours to drive from Bucharest north west towards the Carpathian mountains to Rimnicu-Vilcea. As we drove, the outer suburbs of the city gave way to the small towns and even smaller villages of the countryside. Spring had arrived, and she gave me a glimpse of her beauties. The countryside once trampled underfoot by a régime which sought to destroy it was coming to new life. There is hope, there is a future for everyone, she seemed to be saying to me.

The rainbow colours on some of the wooden houses contrasted with the earth tones of the land. Farmers worked in their fields. There were few cars. Horse-drawn carts laden with hay plodded along slowly as we sped towards our destination. I sat back and soaked into my soul the scenery, the whole experience.

Finally we arrived at Rimnicu-Vilcea. We located the apartment of the director of the orphanage, who was waiting for us, a large, kindly, influential middle-aged mother figure. She joined us in the car and we drove to the home of Simona, the baby's birth mother. We parked outside in a street of endless sameness and drab apartment blocks.

Simona came out to the car while the director of the orphanage stayed in the apartment. Simona's skin was lovely and clear and she had thick, auburn, shoulder-length hair. Over her long, straight, checked skirt she wore a white woven top with a V-neck and three-quarter length sleeves, and she was neat, clean and tidy. I never saw her cry or appear unhappy. Rather, she seemed relieved of a burden.

There was an instant rapport between Simona and me. She said to me, "This child must have a future". I promised her, "I will give this child a future".

There was little sympathy in Romania for women who gave up their children. Simona didn't talk much to anyone, including her parents and younger sister. I felt very sorry for her and assumed that she would go on to get married and have more children. In fact, Gabriel told me that a man in the army wanted to marry her, but she wasn't free to do so until after the adoption of Natasha. Perhaps Simona's intended had not been told of the birth of Natasha because of the prevailing social and cultural standards.

As I approached the orphanage, with Simona walking quickly beside me, there was no overpowering odour of excrement, which was a good sign, unlike some other orphanages. The grounds were clean and tidy. After what seemed like endless cajoling on Simona's part, we managed to get past the female guard stationed in her guard box at the entrance to the orphanage, and entered the grounds.

After the Second World War, Romania became a member of the Eastern Bloc and switched to a communist-style economy. Under Ceausescu's régime the country experienced rapid industrialisation, fuelled by a growing foreign debt, which peaked at $11-12 billion. This was largely paid off during the 1980s by implementing severe austerity measures, which deprived Romanians of basic consumer goods.

After the revolution of 1989, privatisation of industry was pursued. Financial and technical assistance flowed in from the US, the European Union, the International Monetary Fund, the World Bank for Reconstruction and Development and the US Agency for International Development. All these organisations had programmes and resident representatives in Romania.

Despite this, during the harsh economic conditions of the 1990s, some 2.5 million jobs were destroyed. Unprofitable factories were closed down and people began reclaiming the land from which they had been forcibly removed during Ceausescu's regime.

Children of the Decree – a Lost Generation

On October 1 1966, Nicolae Ceausescu enacted Decree 770, which caused untold suffering for women and children. Decree 770 declared abortion and contraception illegal, except for women over forty-five, women who had already borne four children (later raised to five), women whose lives would be in danger if their pregnancy went full term, and women who had conceived due to rape or incest.

In 1966, the population of Romania was approximately nineteen million. With Decree 770, Ceausescu's aim was to increase the population to thirty million by the year 2000, in the belief that population growth would lead to economic growth. By 1976, the population had increased to approximately twenty-one million, an increase of about two million or twelve per cent. Women of childbearing age were subjected to monthly gynaecological examinations to monitor a pregnancy and ensure that an illegal abortion was not carried out. There was a monthly tax on childless people twenty-five years and over, married or not.

Any doctor convicted of an illegal abortion faced a jail term of between ten to twenty years. Despite this, backyard abortions were frequent, resulting in infections, sterility and in some cases, death.

Thousands of babies were abandoned by their impoverished parents into state-run institutions during these dark days of communism between October 1 1966 and December 25 1989, when Ceausescu and his wife Elena were executed by firing squad.

Journalists from around the world descended on Romania, only to discover the horror of these state-run institutions where approximately one hundred thousand children had been abandoned. A journalist whom I met in Brisbane was one of the first to go into Romania after the fall of communism. Approaching an institution, she said she could smell it long before she entered. Children were malnourished, neglected and physically and sexually abused.

Children born during this time were referred to as 'decretei', children of the decree. The word comes from the Romanian word 'decret', meaning decree.

Empty shop shelves and queues for food were common during Communist-era Romania. Lack of food meant that malnourished mothers gave birth to premature and underweight babies. Hospitals fed these babies intravenously with unscreened blood. Hypodermic needles were in short supply and used over and over again without proper sterilisation. As a result of this, more than ten thousand babies were infected with HIV, causing an epidemic of AIDS.

Gabriel told me that Romanians working in state-run orphanages did not like foreigners adopting the children because they feared losing their jobs. There were added benefits to working in orphanages. Truckloads of aid were arriving from Britain. It was said that this aid would go in through one door and out of another; it was never seen in the orphanages. He said that there had previously been 400 babies in this particular orphanage; now there were only 200.

Simona and I walked quickly across a concreted yard until we stood still in front of a large open window, where my baby was being held tightly by a nurse. All my attention was focused on this first meeting with Natasha. It was a scene, like so many from Romania, which remains indelibly printed on my mind.

I reached out and tried to take Natasha in my arms, but the nurse recoiled and held her even more tightly. Natasha sat there quietly in the nurse's arms, alert and sucking her thumb. She seemed to look straight into my very soul with a look that said, "Finally you have arrived. I have been expecting you, waiting for you."

She was clean and chubby-cheeked with beautiful soft, clear skin and deep brown eyes, overhung with long eyelashes. As was the custom, she wore two bonnets. Although she looked chubby, a doctor's report for the court stated that she was malnourished. I learned later that this holding up of babies to the window was normal practice and was the only contact mothers had with their children once they were in the orphanage.

My heart bled for Simona. I thought, "There but for the grace of God go I." Her misfortune was my great good fortune. I thanked God that for whatever reason, Simona had not had an abortion.

This first meeting was over all too quickly before we said goodbye and ran back the way we had come. Gabriel was waiting for us on the street. He watched us coming towards him, Simona talking quickly and excitedly in Romanian, me in English and walking quickly to keep up with her. The joy we shared spread to Gabriel and I can still see the smile on his face as we approached him. I was conscious that my attire was not in keeping with this momentous occasion.

We drove back to Simona's apartment block and walked up half a dozen dingy, dirty flights of stairs to her home. There was no lift. The walls were drab and dirty and needed painting. She shared the tiny one-bedroom apartment in one of the thousands of apartment blocks with a younger sister and brother and their mother and father. The brother was not there, but I knew I was privileged to meet the rest of her family. So many adoptive parents knew nothing of their child's birth family and had no way of finding information.

The beds were all neatly made and lined up against the drab walls of the long bedroom. There was one double bed, for the parents, and two single beds. There was a tiny gap in the middle of the room where you could stand to make the beds or get dressed, and Simona's brother and sister and parents slept there.

An enclosed veranda big enough for drying clothes, opened

out from the living room. The living room furniture consisted of a couch, wardrobe, TV, table and chairs. There was a bathroom with a hand basin and bath and a separate toilet. I did not see the kitchen.

There would be much I could share with Natasha as she grew up, if and when she wanted to know. I would be proud to talk to her about her birth family. They were good, wholesome, down-to-earth people. They were victims of their circumstances, of the time and place they were born.

We stayed about ten minutes, with everyone talking excitedly and genuinely pleased to see me. Then Gabriel and I left with the director of the orphanage and returned to her apartment. It was spacious with two or three bedrooms and boasted beautiful furniture.

After freshening up in the bathroom, where there was actually hot running water from the basin and toilet paper beside the toilet, we were served delicate pastries, cake, wine and Turkish coffee at a lovely dining-room table. I wanted to linger and savour every mouthful, but Gabriel was anxious to leave.

I was warm in the car, at peace and quietly content. We arrived back in Bucharest at 3.30 pm, and I had to use my last $US30 to pay the driver. Translating my documents and accommodation had used up the remainder of my funds.

It was an Easter tradition of Michaela's to make walnut cakes. She used elongated, expanding cake tins so the cakes were quite long. The kitchen was square, with a sink in the left-hand corner as you walked in through the open doorway. To the right was a kitchen table where all the food preparation was done as there was not enough bench space.

I sat at the table and helped Michaela by shelling and

finely chopping the walnuts for her Easter cakes. There was a large modern refrigerator and a big window letting in lots of light. The old stove was gas and not all the elements worked properly. Everything, apart from the fridge, was old.

The kitchen was near the back door, which led out on to the back yard. On the way down the garden path to the back shed you passed a well, enclosed with blue ceramic tiles. There were always large old cooking pots sitting there. A clothes line hung across the front of the garden shed.

Gabriel walked down the garden path towards me. I was sitting in front of the garden shed, writing in my diary. It was a beautiful, calm, spring day with warmth in the air.

"What are you writing?" he asked.

"I'm writing about you," I replied. Saying nothing, Gabriel turned and walked into the kitchen. His business that afternoon was not with me.

According to the Christian tradition the Archangel Gabriel, believed to be God's messenger, was used by God to announce to the Virgin Mary that she would conceive a child by the Holy Spirit. This is known as the Annunciation. This Gabriel, whose mother was called Mary, was facilitating modern day miracles of his own. He made extraordinary things happen in the lives of ordinary people. As if divinely inspired, he decided which child would be given to which mother. The symbolism of these events was not lost on me.

My parents' corner store, Dunedin, New Zealand

Natasha's passport photo

Natasha as a toddler after we moved to Brisbane

With Natasha (left) and Melannie

Communist Romania before the Revolution

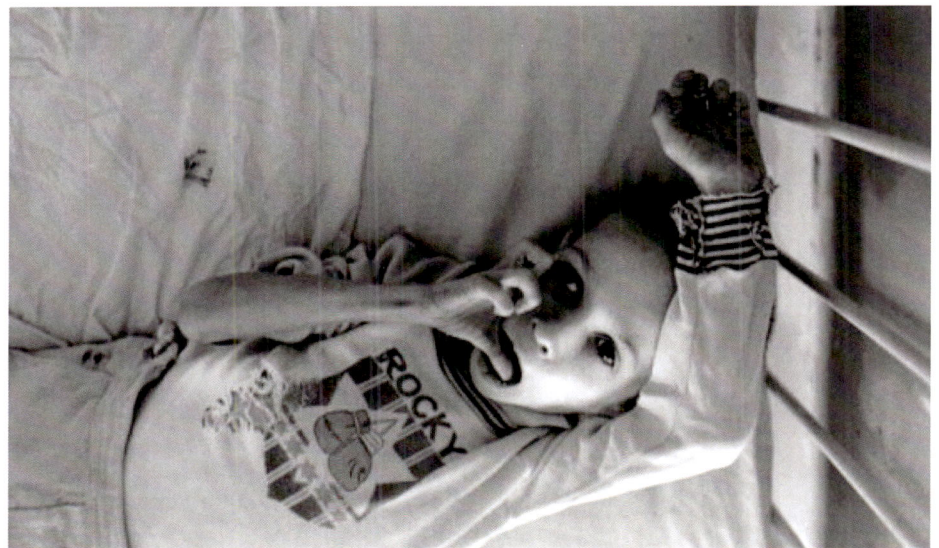

A young child confined to a crib, Sighetu Marmatiei Institute for the Unsalvageables, Romania 1992, © Thomas B. Szalay. Sighetu Marmatiei is a small town in Transylvania at Romania's northern border with Ukraine. The institute was opened in 1973 and closed in 2003. Hundreds of children died here during that time.

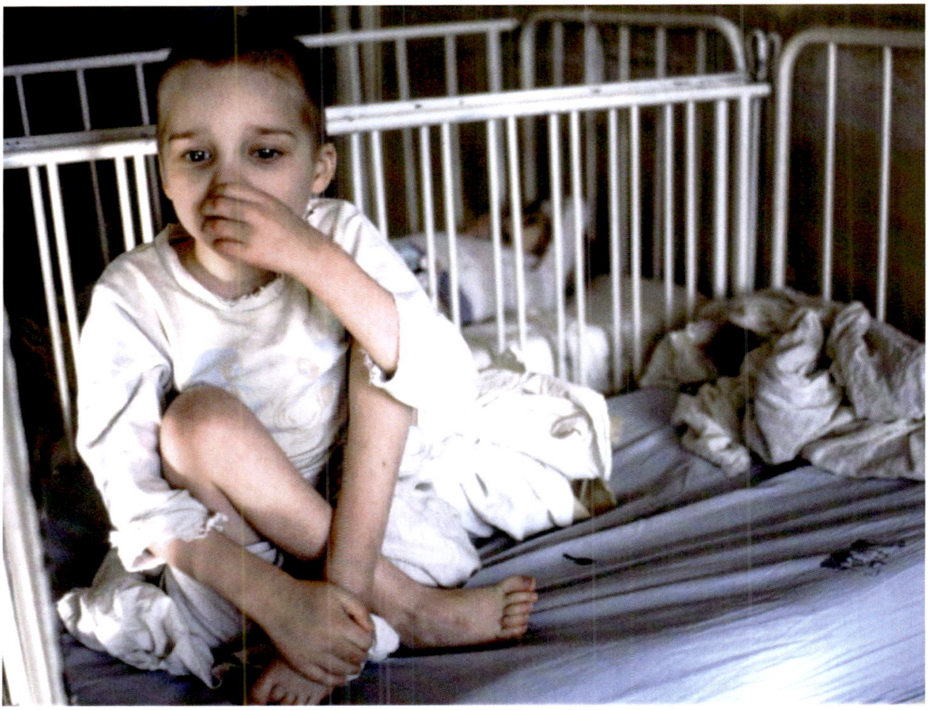

A malnourished and neglected child sitting cross-legged in a crib in the Sighetu Marmatiei Institute for the Unsalvageables. © Thomas B. Szalay

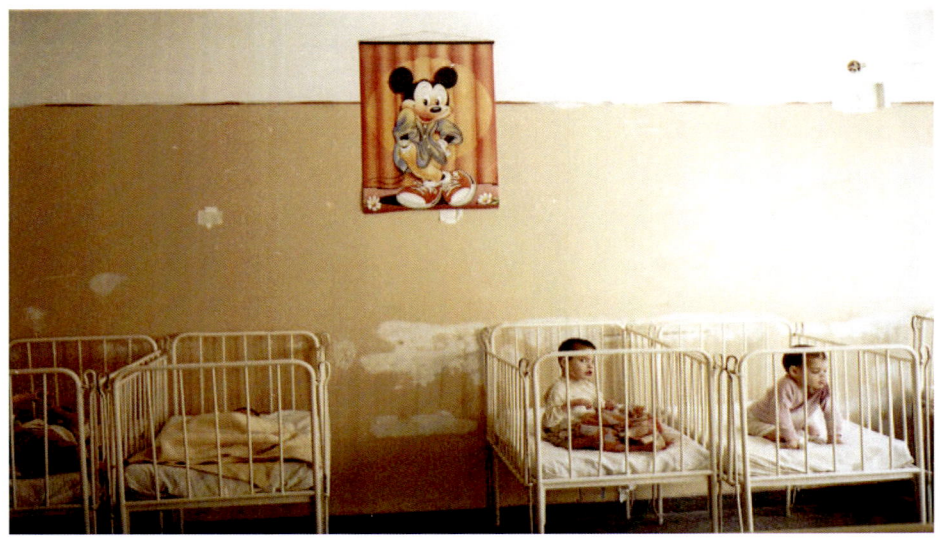

Children confined to cots with a poster of Mickey Mouse above them, Sighetu Marmatiei Institute. © Thomas B. Szalay

Head-shaven girls waiting to start eating breakfast. Single pane window, concrete floors, very chilly inside and all the kids had to wear were rags. Sighetu Marmatiei Institute, © Thomas B. Szalay

Children looking out from the windows of the Sighetu Marmatiei Institute.
© Thomas B. Szalay

Locked gate of the Sighetu
Marmatiei Institute, © Thomas B. Szalay

Bucharest Street, 2015
© Thomas B. Szalay

Izidor Ruckel, a voice for the abandoned children of Romania, sitting in the ruins of the Institute. Izidor lived here from three years of age until eleven, when he was adopted by an American couple. Abandoned for Life is Izidor's memoir of the horrors of the Institute.

© Thomas B. Szalay

Traditional haymaking, Romanian countryside,

2015 © Thomas B. Szalay

Old lady spinning wool the traditional way,
Romanian countryside 2015. © Thomas B. Szalay

The author, Adele Rickerby

CHAPTER SEVEN

The mornings were bad, not knowing what lay ahead each day. I walked up and down the street where I lived. It was an old, potholed, cobbled street in one of the few remaining pockets of single dwellings left in Bucharest. Ceausescu had large numbers of houses destroyed to make way for apartment block boxes.

This systematic destruction of houses in towns and villages was part of the Romanian government's programme for systemisation, which proposed radical restructuring of the infrastructure of towns and villages. This included the destruction of historic churches and monasteries. People who were brave enough to speak out against the régime were arrested, imprisoned, tortured and sometimes murdered. One such person, who became an enemy of the communist régime, was the brave priest Laszlo Tokes. He preached sermons to his congregation denouncing the communist régime's abuses of human rights.

On March 3, 1989, Laszlo Tokes was ordered to stop

preaching to his congregation in Timisoara. Orders were given for him to be evicted from his church flat. His power was cut off and his ration book was taken away, but his parishioners continued to support and provision him. The state had some supporters arrested and beaten.

As December 15 approached, Lazslo Tokes was still in his flat with his parishioners keeping vigil. From here, the crowds grew until the vigil turned into a revolt against the Romanian régime. Two days later, the army fired into the crowd, causing numerous casualties. Tens of thousands of industrial workers in Timisoara took to the streets. The protests quickly spread across Romania, escalating into the Romanian Revolution of 1989 which overthrew Ceausescu and his communist régime.

As I slowly walked down the street past the humble homes of these ordinary people, I reflected that they were the lucky few with homes to call their own. Small grassy patches and garden beds were evident. Some backyards had hens to supplement their owners' frugal diets with fresh eggs. Some had small vegetable patches where I could see an early spring growth of lettuces, shallots and radishes, which would be welcome after the long, hard winter without fresh fruit or vegetables.

CHAPTER EIGHT

I waited for Mrs Contescu to arrange to have Natasha removed from the orphanage and taken back to her birth mother's apartment. We would then be able to take her from there to the hospital to have the blood tests for Hepatitis B and AIDS. I was 99.9% sure in my heart that Natasha was healthy and that she had not been a victim of the practice of using unscreened blood in transfusions with infected, unsterilised needles which have been used multiple times because of a shortage. But we had to proceed with the tests anyway.

Arriving at Simona's apartment, I found it a tiny space of intense feeling and activity. Natasha was lying peacefully on the couch in the living room, mesmerised by the TV. I was able to hold her for the first time. She was serene and beautiful, albeit soaking wet. There were no nappies for her. Fortunately I had brought a supply of disposable nappies, formula and baby clothes.

Her grandmother supervised me while I changed her into clean clothes and put a nappy on her. She showed me how she had been feeding Natasha with dry biscuits soaked in freshly-squeezed apple juice and boiled cows' milk fed to her via a glass Coke bottle with a teat attached to it. The grandmother acted proudly and confidently.

Natasha was well wrapped against the fresh spring air as we left the apartment for the hospital where the blood tests were to be taken. After some time waiting in a clinic room, two middle-aged, kind and considerate nurses appeared. I was there to hold Natasha, to ensure that the sterile, disposable needles we had brought with us were used, that there were two separate bottles of blood, one for HIV and one for Hepatitis B, and that it was definitely her blood that we had.

On returning to the tiny apartment, we were served what was by their standards a lavish meal, which Natasha's grandmother had gone to much trouble and expense to prepare. Photos were taken, jokes told and toasts made. It was late in the evening by the time we finally arrived back in Bucharest.

The next morning dawned dismal and wet and I donned my grey overcoat. Two vials of blood, stored in the fridge overnight, were placed safely in one pocket. I walked until I found a taxi to take me to the Institute of Virology, where the tests for AIDS and Hepatitis B would be done. Once there, with difficulty, I located the laboratory and knocked at the door. It was opened by an angry English-speaking doctor who harangued me about the poor state of the laboratory and the lack of facilities. Behind him, sitting at a table in the middle of the dimly-lit room, smoking and talking, were two women wearing white uniforms.

"I should have closed it down months ago" said the doctor. He said he could not guarantee me negative results; 20%

of all the blood tested from Rimnicu-Vilcea was coming up positive for AIDS. I held back tears as I gave him the blood in exchange for a number. Then I turned to walk back down the staircase.

I could no longer contain my sadness. I sat on the empty stairs of the dilapidated building and cried. You could have washed the filthy floor with my tears. I cried, not because I was afraid that Natasha would have AIDS or Hepatitis B, because in my heart I knew she hadn't and this was just a formality. I cried for the innocent babies who lay dying of AIDS, unloved and uncared for. I cried for the loss of my naivety. No amount of overseas travel could have prepared me for what I had encountered in Romania.

Eventually, I composed myself and found a taxi to take me home.

Despite every Friday afternoon being a half-day holiday, the doctor assured me that I could return at 2 pm to the Institute of Virology to collect the results. This I duly did, and they were negative. Now I could collect my baby and proceed to the next step of the adoption process.

I awoke to a beautiful spring morning and the promise of new life and hope for the future. As Gabriel and I left the city, we passed by ancient buildings, their walls covered in a profusion of purple wisteria. Once again we drove along rugged, potholed roads between forests and farmhouses, north-west to Rimnicu-Vilcea at the foothills of the Carpathian mountains. There wasn't constant chatter between Gabriel and myself. We were comfortable in each other's silence.

Eventually Gabriel and I arrived at the apartment. There was a small couch to the left of the room as you stepped inside the door, and Natasha was lying there. She was so serene waiting for me, and I was lost in the moment. I didn't take any notice of who else was in the tiny, drab apartment.

Gabriel stood behind me and leaned forward to look at Natasha, who was wrapped in several shawls. I picked her up and clutched her tightly to me. We left quickly and Gabriel walked closely behind me as we descended the dingy stairs. He opened the car door for me. Sitting in the seclusion of the back seat of the car, Natasha huddled in my arms, slept soundly. My long-held dream was finally fulfilled. I cried.

Gabriel said, "You've got a strange way of showing you're happy."

CHAPTER NINE

After three weeks, no longer able to cope with the overcrowded, difficult conditions at Michaela's house, I gratefully took up the offer of Gabriel's apartment. Here I had the peace and solitude I needed. It was private and there was plenty of hot water in the mornings and evenings. It was warm and I had full use of the stove to heat water for formula. There was a grill which I used to grill cheese on hard, round bread.

Gabriel gave up his bed for me and slept on the living-room couch. There was an old-fashioned wicker Moses basket for Natasha, given to me by a kind-hearted stranger. Natasha slept cosily and peacefully in the basket, which sat on the floor, comfortably close to my bed. There was a small clothes cupboard in a corner of the room; the door to it would never shut properly. A small, silver cross hung on the wall above the bed. On the wall opposite, there was a peaceful picture of a quaint country scene with a peasant girl sitting quietly beside a stream, reminiscent of a Constable landscape.

A small fridge the size of a bar fridge stood in an alcove

off the hallway in Gabriel's tiny apartment. After I moved in I opened it, only to find it was empty, so I started making a list of all the food we needed. Gabriel said that was a waste of time, because there weren't supermarkets or shops where you could just go and buy what you wanted. The shops only had what was available. All I saw in one shop were lots of tins of black caviar, many different flavours of cordial, and jars of cream for chilblains.

When Natasha smiled, she smiled with her whole body, her mouth opening wide. Her arms and legs moved in pleasurable response. She was more alert with each passing day, and more restless. She slept well for a few hours in the morning and surprisingly well at night time, but was restless all afternoon and in the early evening.

One day not long after Natasha and I had arrived at his apartment, Gabriel went to the clinic where he worked – he managed to work, as well as processing adoptions. After he had gone there was a knock at the door. I opened it to find an old lady standing there, holding a metal canister of stew. I went to give her some money, but she didn't take it and left. When Gabriel came home, I told him of this incident. It was one of the rare occasions when I saw him smile. He thought it was a great joke, because the old woman with the food was Mary, his mother.

I was beginning to turn the tiny apartment into a laundry. Nappies and items of clothing hung over a line strung down the narrow corridor and drying over a chair in front of the heater. There was hot water every morning and I was able to shower, wash my hands and do the dishes. There was no water at all during the day, hot or cold, so I collected what I needed for the day in every available kitchen container. Even the toilet did not flush after a certain time in the morning.

As I waited for the social worker in Rimnicu-Vilcea to complete a home study of Natasha's birth family, I reflected how much I missed Melannie. It was the first time we had been separated, except for one week in hospital when I had the hysterectomy. Yet I was thankful for this time when there was just Natasha and me. I could concentrate on getting to know her, on nurturing her, without the added demands of a six-year-old daughter, a husband and a house to look after. It was an important time of bonding.

There was an instant, heartfelt connection with Natasha, as if it was meant to be.

I also needed to rest and renew my energy for the difficult and demanding journey still ahead of me. I grieved a little for the first four months of Natasha's life, the part I had not been able to share.

On fine days, with Natasha securely snuggled in a pouch (another item given to me by a kind-hearted stranger), we ventured into the city and I absorbed its sights, smells and sounds. There was a shop where I could buy disposable nappies, chocolate and biscuits. Several hotel foyers were meeting places for other adoptive parents from Ireland, England, New Zealand, America and Canada.

Walking towards one such hotel, I was accosted by a Romanian who was standing on the steps in front of the hotel, watching me approach. "Can I buy your baby?" he asked me in English. I was outraged and could not find enough words, or the right words, to express my anger, so I remained silent. I had been told that the going rate for a baby on the black market was US$20,000, which was what American couples were willing to pay.

Spring brought with it a restlessness and excitement which stirred these long-silent, suppressed people to voice their frustrations. Each day, in ever-increasing numbers, they gathered in the city square, where one could still see reminders of the 1989 revolution in empty, barricaded, bullet-ridden buildings. Someone had placed a simple wooden cross in the square, and people were constantly adorning this with spring bulbs. The power of the people prevailed. Lest we forget.

Early one fine, Saturday morning, Natasha and I took a taxi to the park. Before venturing in, I breakfasted at a nearby restaurant on fried eggs, toast, cheese, salami, strong black coffee and orange juice.

Natasha and I were the only ones there. The staff made a fuss of us and Natasha was nursed the whole time I was having my meal. I felt I was on display, my every move examined closely, questioningly. Breakfast cost 820 lei. They asked for dollars, but I had only a $10 note. I was afraid I would not be given change.

The park, Cismigiu Gardens, was full of people enjoying the sun on that weekend morning. No one else had a baby in a pouch. We were accosted by a brightly-dressed young gypsy woman who asked for money. Her companion was holding a baby, tightly bound. They were persistent and followed me, but I refused to give them any money. Finally, they left. Other women stopped to smile at Natasha, say hello or tell me off because she wasn't wearing at least one bonnet. Natasha hated bonnets and I couldn't keep them on her head. She always managed to pull them off.

The spring freshness of the morning, of new growth and activity in the park, contrasted with the dirt and decay of the city. Rubbish was left to pile up, roads were in disrepair, old buildings were falling down, new ones half-completed were vacant, the workmen idle. There was no money to finish them.

CHAPTER TEN

At last, the busy social worker had written a report on Simona's family circumstances for the judge, and a court date had been set. Simona and I had to appear in front of the judge at the courthouse in Rimnicu-Vilcea, where Natasha had been born on December 16, 1990. Before the introduction of the Central Adoption Commission, Romanian District Courts were able to approve all adoptions.

The courthouse corridors were packed with a mingling mass of people dressed in brown and black, the just and the unjust walking and waiting together. Gabriel and I sat on a hard wooden seat as we anxiously waited.

Finally it was our turn. We walked to the top of a wooden staircase and were ushered into a large room. The room was devoid of furniture, except for a desk behind which a middle-aged judge sat, looking at my file. Simona was already in the room, standing to the left of me. It seemed to me that she just wanted it all over and done with. The judge, very much the pillar of society, looked contemptuously at Simona, as if she had been a bad girl. No sympathy there. Instead, he seemed to be mocking her. The judge was being judgemental. He spoke to her briefly, tersely. Simona answered back, briefly but in Romanian of course, so I couldn't understand what she said.

The judge turned towards me. The agonising moment of decision-making had arrived. I held my breath, my stomach tensed.

Within minutes it was over. The judge had allowed the adoption to go ahead. Simona ran quickly out of the courtroom and down the stairs. Gabriel and I walked downstairs to a room where the court proceedings were written up and translated into English. The investigation by the busy, overworked social worker revealed that the mother did not work and that she did not have any income for maintaining the child in a house which the child's grandparent's rented from the State, the flat being made up of two rooms. The minor is the daughter out of wedlock, it read, and since the mother had no possibility to care for the child, she consented to the adoption of the child.

It was there, at the District Court, that I was soon to discover I had made a terrible mistake, one which had the potential to lead to disaster.

> Session of the Council Chamber of 6.V.1991
>
> There is judged the application formulated by spouses BURGESS ANTHONY WILLIAM AND BURGESS ADELE FRANCIS, foreign citizens residing in 169 Jensen St, Edge Hill, Cairns, Queensland, Australia, for the consent of adoption of minor .... Present before the court were the adopter Burgess Adele Francis, with power of attorney for her husband Anthony William and attended by translator Melnic Gabriel, mother of minor and tutelar authority.

Procedure legally fulfilled.

Translator M.G. for applicants asked the admission of action and consent of adoption of minor with full effects. Mother of minor, agreed with adoption. The representative of tutelar authority and that of the prosecutor's office asked for consent of adoption, all legal conditions being fulfilled.

The adopters have deposited papers of which result that they can adopt according to the laws in their country, they have material possibilities, have no criminal records and their health is good. Analysing the evidence of the file the Court notes that all legal conditions are fulfilled and noting that the adoption is made to the interest of the child, with full effects, according to art. 78 1 Family Code the adopted child will bear after the adoption the name of Burgess.

FOR THESE REASONS ON BEHALF OF LAW THE COURT DECIDES

Admits the application formulated by spouses Burgess Anthony William and Burgess Adele Frances, above address, and consequently:

Admits the adoption with full effects of minor by spouses Burgess Anthony William (b. 27.12.1950) and Burgess Adele Francis (b.10.01.1957) above address; The minor will bear after adoption the name of Burgess. With appeal in 15 days since communication.

Issued on 6 May 1991 at the Vilcea County Court. DECREE ABSOLUTE through not resorting to appeal. signatures Chairman - Judge - Clerk SEAL COURT.

I have included information about the court proceedings of the adoption in order to dispel the rumours and innuendo that the adoption was in any way illegal or that money changed hands, leading to the assumption that I had "bought" Natasha from her birth mother. Tragically, the illegal adoptions and human trafficking of abandoned babies and children in institutions and intact families, led to the Romanian government having to bring in a Moratorium on International Adoptions.

Gabriel had business to attend to in a remote village beyond Rimnicu-Vilcea, so once the paperwork was completed we journeyed through the picturesque spring countryside to the village. This was a very poor village with no paved roads or footpaths. I couldn't see any electricity cables or plumbing.

Gabriel told me that the women of the village would wash their clothes in a nearby stream. In the winter, he said, the ground and the hovels the villages called home would be covered in snow. It would be bitterly cold. Wolves would prowl close to the village and howl menacingly.

On arrival, our car was immediately surrounded by curious children. I had a packet of biscuits with me and started dishing them out to the children, one by one. The bolder children came back for more, the shyer ones held back. Gabriel got tired of it and told me to quickly give them the whole packet.

When Gabriel's discussions with a couple in the village had ended, we turned and headed back through the mountains to Bucharest. I had left Natasha early that morning with a babysitter, but I was missing her terribly and anxious to get back.

What a terrible day, one of the worst. I left early in the morning to go to the bank to get the extra money I had had sent over about four weeks ago, $600. I needed it to buy my ticket out from Bucharest to Frankfurt and to pay for several nights' accommodation while I was in Germany organising visas. Germany is very expensive.

When I asked for my money, the lady teller told me it wasn't there. I didn't believe her. She had lied to me once before, saying my money wasn't there, and when I pressed her further, she had looked at the ledgers and found an entry for it. So this time I assumed she was lying again. But she emphatically repeated that the $600 wasn't there. She was very sorry, there was nothing she could do.

I made such a fuss. I insisted on seeing the bank manager, and was ushered into an adjoining office; everyone was watching. Two ladies in the office checked and rechecked, made phone calls, but there was no record of my money having arrived. Yet I knew it had been sent and had the telegraphic transfer numbers. In the end, there was nothing I or anyone else could do. My $600 had gone missing in transit.

I was stranded in Bucharest, after being there for six weeks, adoption formalities completed, but no money. I didn't have a credit card. I had gone all that way without one, a foolish mistake. I had a connecting flight to catch in Düsseldorf to take me to Tokyo, then Sydney, where I was to meet Melannie, then on to Auckland and Wellington.

I was devastated. If only I had gone to the bank weeks before, I thought. I would have known the money wasn't there sooner, and it would have given time for more to be sent over.

I returned to Gabriel's apartment exhausted, desolate, and feeling very let down. Once again, Gabriel came to my rescue. He gave me the $600. I viewed it as a temporary loan until I could get back home and send him the money. But by now, after having been let down many times, Gabriel's faith in human nature was all but shattered. He gave me the money without expecting it back again. I was deeply grateful for his generosity. Now I was able to buy my ticket on Tarom Airlines, and get a visa from the German Embassy for Germany. It was a simple matter to obtain a visa for Germany from the German embassy in Bucharest. I planned to travel to Bonn, where there were New Zealand and Australian embassies where I could get more visas.

CHAPTER ELEVEN

The day dawned fine, but my heart had clouded over. I had to leave Romania. I only had one pair of hands. I was very limited in what I could carry. I had to leave behind the dear friends I had made. All I could take with me were precious memories of their care and kindness towards me.

Natasha, sleeping serenely in her cane baby basket, was oblivious to my preparations for our journey together. Gabriel, hands in pockets, stood and watched. He was concerned that I would pack too much. He kept urging me to hurry up. He was afraid I would miss the flight.

I walked around his tiny apartment for the last time. I was very reluctant to leave its safety and sanctuary. I didn't want to travel on my own through Germany for four days from Bucharest to Wellington with a baby, but I had to. During the last six weeks, no one, friend, family or husband, had arrived to help me. I missed Melannie in a way only a mother could. I longed to see her. I longed to cuddle her. I longed to introduce her to her new baby sister. My love for her spurred me on.

As Gabriel drove us the short distance to the airport, we passed a group of gypsy women wearing long, dirty skirts. They were repairing the pot-holed road with thick black tar.

I entered the airport with a heavy heart. There wasn't much time left now. Gabriel checked in my suitcase. Silently, people walked past us on their way to their destinations. Gabriel and I, as newly-formed friends do, exchanged the usual promises. He would come and visit me in Australia and I would come back and visit him in Romania. But these were promises neither of us were destined to keep. He held himself back from me and I from him as we quickly said our goodbyes.

I walked towards customs. There was a nerve-racking hitch at passport control. I could see the plane on the runway in front of me, but I was held up. My visa for Romania had run out after four weeks and I had not renewed it because it was a difficult and complex task. Of course, the young official at passport control was not at all happy, and I stood there praying, holding back tears, thinking I could not cope with further complications and looking down at my beautiful baby. I told him that the adoption had taken longer than I had anticipated, trying to appeal to his compassion.

He fidgeted with papers, looking embarrassed and awkward, while the queue behind me grew longer and longer. I had no Romanian money to pay for another visa and nothing I could bribe him with.

Then he looked away and date-stamped my passport. I was free to go. I had been waiting less than five minutes, but it felt like an eternity.

CHAPTER TWELVE

I was not looking forward to being in Germany on my own with Natasha for the next four days. I felt very alone and even more vulnerable now, with a dependant four-month-old baby. What if either of us were to get sick? What if I couldn't get somewhere to stay? Bonn was a very difficult place in which to find accommodation. What if, for some reason, my onward tickets weren't available in Frankfurt, or weren't paid for, or the dates were wrong? How would I manage by myself with a baby in a pouch, needing bottles and changing, a handbag and a suitcase? How would I even be able to go to the toilet?

The journey on Tarom from Bucharest to Frankfurt was, thankfully, only two hours. Conditions were cramped. There were many other foreigners, German and Canadian, returning home to new lives with babies, toddlers and children.

I sat beside a middle-aged man returning to Canada with a toddler. His wife had left earlier. We helped each other and he bought me a most delicious and expensive lunch at Frankfurt airport; vegetable soup, fresh rolls with butter. I savoured every mouthful. We parted, he to a connecting flight – he would be back home within 24 hours – and I to a hotel room which I had booked at the airport.

After a long wait a small van arrived, to take me and other guests to our hotel. It was very clean and civilised and close to the railway station. But it was only a B&B, so once I was settled in I reluctantly had to venture out into the night to find food. My surroundings seemed vaguely familiar. I had been in Germany in early 1978, aged 22, 13 years earlier, as part of a short holiday around Europe after completing my three-and-a-half-year general nursing course in Dunedin, New Zealand.

After breakfast the next morning, I left my luggage in the lobby and walked across the square to the JAL and Air New Zealand offices to collect my onward tickets.

Frankfurt, so prosperous and sparsely populated, was a huge culture shock after a journey of only two hours from Bucharest, from one extreme to the other. I could not reconcile myself to this. It was so unfair. I wanted to take all the contents of all the shops back to Bucharest and give them out for free. Or to let people from Bucharest loose in the supermarkets, restaurants and shops.

Walking through the square, I came across a fruit stall with brightly-coloured canopies. Unbelievably, it sold apples from New Zealand – crisp, red, perfect, juicy apples. I bought apples, bananas and oranges. I was so grateful. It was the first fresh fruit I had eaten in six weeks.

After collecting my onward flight tickets, I returned to the hotel lobby for my luggage, then Natasha and I took a train to Bonn.

In Bonn, I felt alone with my loneliness and my fears. I could not allow myself to despair and had to continue to be positive and calmly think things through. Natasha slept opposite me, blissfully unaware of all the drama she was causing.

It was a dreadful day in Bonn, miserable and overcast, reflecting my mood. The hotel, the Astoria, fortunately had a vacancy for that night at least. It is always difficult to find accommodation in that city.

But at the New Zealand embassy I found that I had made a stupid mistake. I had forgotten to get the Citizenship B form filled in before leaving Romania. The notarised copy of the court proceedings, translated, might not be enough. So now I was sitting here by myself, waiting and wondering whether or not I would get a visa for New Zealand for Natasha tomorrow morning and, if not, what in heaven's name I was going to do. I was hoping they would forget about their bureaucracy and allow me a visa on humanitarian grounds. Sounds naïve, doesn't it? But I didn't know what to do. I vacillated between thinking positively and preparing for the worst. The embassy needed overnight approval from New Zealand. It's not as if I was adopting Natasha illegally, but if they didn't give me a visa it was as if they were saying as much. I decided to report there first thing and throw myself on their mercy.

I had a cup of coffee and fetched more hot water for the Thermos flask I had bought in Frankfurt to provide boiled water for Natasha's formula. I walked to the bakery for some delicious pastries and went across the road to the cathedral to pray.

Lucky once again. I arrived at the New Zealand embassy at 9 am, prepared for the worst, to be told I needed the Citizenship B form but I could get it filled in at the Romanian

Embassy by the Romanian Consular General. The Romanian Embassy was only open Mondays, Wednesdays and Fridays, but today was Wednesday, so I was in luck. I rushed down there by taxi.

As I pushed my way through the crowd of people waiting outside the embassy, people were looking at me. I was an oddity, a thin, foreign, fair-haired lady carrying a baby in a pouch. Someone I had met in Romania told me that at the different embassies in Europe mothers with babies were given priority, especially if the babies were crying. This was a very useful piece of information, which I now put to the test.

It worked. No one stopped me as I pushed my way to the front of the crowd, and I entered the doors of the small embassy. Ahead of me I could see the counter. Behind it, several officials with bewildered, overwhelmed looks on their faces were coming and going from a closed office to the left. There was another crowd of people, men and women, between me and the officials. I was the only person with a baby. The crowd filled up the small embassy. Once again, I was able to push through to the counter without being stopped by someone who might have been waiting for hours. Once again, strangers had shown kindness towards me.

I explained to the official what I needed. I waited 15 minutes, pacing up and down all the time. Going back to the official, I made a fuss, asking how much longer it would be.

Finally the Romanian Consular General came out of the office and handed me a notarised Citizenship B Form. With a big smile on his face, he wished me good luck.

I rushed back by taxi to the New Zealand Embassy, where I quickly got Natasha's visa. Then I went on to the Australian Embassy, with half an hour to spare before it closed for the day at midday, to get a transit visa for Natasha. We would be stopping in Australia en route to New Zealand, waiting in the transit lounge in Sydney for several hours. At Sydney Airport I would meet Melannie, so we could all travel together to New Zealand.

The visas, taxis and hotel cost a fortune, but that didn't matter. In fact I ordered a hot lunch at a restaurant to celebrate. It was delicious, a nutritious salad, fluffy omelette with bacon. It was the first hot meal I'd had in days. I accidentally knocked over Natasha's bottle of formula onto the fresh, clean checked tablecloth while I was waiting for it to cool down.

I returned to the hotel where I had left my luggage in the foyer and changed Natasha on top of the toilet seat in a tiny toilet cubicle. There was no room on the floor. Then I caught a taxi to the station to take a train to Düsseldorf. I arrived at the station just as the train was leaving, so the taxi driver helped me aboard and said I could pay for my ticket once I was on the train.

It was overcast and raining on and off all day. I feared one of us would catch a cold, even though Natasha was cocooned and covered in her pouch and wearing a purple beanie which she kept trying to take off. She was so good. It was as if in her spirit she knew and understood what was happening. She took it all in her stride. We were constantly together. I never left her, even to go to the toilet.

CHAPTER THIRTEEN

In Düsseldorf I found a lonely, depressing hotel room. There was no lift, so I had to carry my suitcase up several flights of stairs. I was thankful for a quiet place to rest. My room looked out onto the rain and rooftops of the city.

I bought Melannie a small gift of chocolate. I could not believe I would be seeing her again soon. I had missed her terribly. I had a bad dream that I went to find her and couldn't, but when I got home she turned up, unperturbed. I had wanted her to have a sister, and Natasha would be that sister.

I finally allowed myself a measure of relief as I boarded the plane for Tokyo via a stopover in Anchorage. I do not travel well at the best of times, easily getting seasick, carsick or airsick, but all went well with the flight until we were near Tokyo. I feel sick thinking about it even now. Despite wearing wrist pressure bands which I found helpful on the way over, as we approached Tokyo, we experienced a lot of turbulence and the sickness began to overwhelm me. I applied a transdermal patch behind my ear, but it was no help.

My responsibility for Natasha's wellbeing and safety weighed heavily. How would I cope? How would I be able to look after her if I was sick? How could I look after myself? The turbulence increased; it was some of the worst I had ever experienced. Feeling terrible and already weary after the traumas of Bucharest and the long flight, I had to make use of the sick bags provided. Fortunately, Natasha was quiet and safe and did not need my attention.

I started to worry that I would be too unwell to continue my journey on to Sydney, where Melannie was waiting for us. Perhaps we would have to rest overnight in Tokyo and make alternative arrangements. I prayed, beginning to feel as if Jesus was carrying Natasha and me in His arms. I was exhausted and felt I couldn't go a step further on my journey, even though Melannie, whom I hadn't seen for six weeks, was waiting for me in Sydney.

Feeling secure and comforted and relying on His strength, we eventually landed and disembarked. As we left the plane, a hostess commented that it was the worst turbulence she had ever experienced flying into Tokyo.

I had six hours to wait before boarding my flight to Sydney and my daughter. I longed to show her her new sister. I used the time to sit quietly, eat a little and refresh myself and Natasha. I enjoyed making conversation with English-speaking people in the busy airport.

My excitement at the prospect of seeing Melannie took over and sustained me on this leg of the journey, but I worried that something had gone wrong and she wouldn't be there at the airport waiting for me. I was anxious and disappointed when, after landing, I couldn't find her. I made enquiries and learned that, yes, there was confusion over flight times etc. and she had arrived yesterday, a day early, but was due to return any minute. I felt for her, waiting and waiting yesterday and going home empty handed.

I paced up and down, looking at all the doors and cars as they arrived. At last I spotted her, with my sister-in-law Ruth. I thought, is that my daughter? she looked so much like me. I hadn't realised it before. We fell onto the floor in a heap of cuddles, kisses and tears.

"I made it!" I said to Ruth, who had given up her time to travel from Brisbane with Melannie. We had only a short time together before Melannie, Natasha and I had to board the flight to Auckland.

Changing flights in Auckland for the last leg of the journey to Wellington, we went to the toilet at the terminal. The door locked shut, locking us all in, and there was nobody around to help. Fortunately there was a gap between the top of the door and the roof. Melannie managed to climb up and through this gap to unlock the door from the outside. We had just enough time to walk across the tarmac to our connecting flight to Wellington.

Alena was waiting for us at Wellington airport. I said to her, "I made it!"

I enjoyed the quiet and peaceful domesticity of Alena's home, with its rituals and routines. My father and my eldest sister, Fiona, visited briefly from Dunedin. My mother-in-law also called in, from Christchurch. They all had turns holding Natasha, who thrived on all the attention.

During all the celebrations, no one had the courage to ask the question which remained unanswered: "Where is your husband?" They all knew of the difficulties we had experienced in our relationship over the years, and that he had chosen not to go to Romania with me. He could have taken time off work, as his mother was already in Cairns looking after Melannie whilst I was away. He had not flown with Melannie from Cairns to Brisbane, then Brisbane to Sydney. Instead he had put her, at six years of age, on a plane by herself for the flight to Brisbane. She had vomited on the flight down and he hadn't packed a change of clothing, so she had left the plane wrapped in a blanket.

Ruth had met Melannie at Brisbane airport and accompanied her on the journey to Sydney, where they had stayed overnight with friends. Melannie just took all this in her stride, and never complained.

Alena took me into the city to get Natasha's New Zealand citizenship by descent and her New Zealand passport, so that I could fly with her into Australia. I could not believe how easy that was. By that time, though, I was over paperwork, procedures and protocols, and Alena admonished me for being unnecessarily rude to the nice, helpful public servants we encountered. The New Zealand government's humanitarian approach towards Romania's orphans was in stark contrast to the Australian government's. Obviously, the New Zealand government knew these children were not going to be reunited with the parents, who had abandoned them for reasons of poverty. By contrast, as stated in the Australian Minister for Immigration's letter, the Australian government lied and said all these 100,000 abandoned children would be reunited with their families when economic conditions in Romania improved.

After ten days of domestic bliss, rest and recovery at my sister's, Melannie, Natasha and I finally arrived in Cairns. I had been away for two months. Tony finally met Natasha, then went to work.

In July 1991, only two months after my arrival back in Cairns, an article in the *Cairns Post* caught my attention. It was titled "Romania Halts All Adoptions". The article explained that due to widespread corruption, the then president, Ion Iliescu, had signed a law halting all adoptions until new adoption legislation could be implemented. The article stated that the most disturbing of these corrupt practices was the selling of babies on the black market for as much as $US25,000. A significant change to the adoption process would be the processing of all adoptions through the newly-formed Romanian Adoption Committee instead of the district courts. Since the December 1989 anti-communist revolution, when worldwide media highlighted the plight of the 100,000 babies and children abandoned in appalling conditions throughout Romania, some 5000 of these children had been adopted by Westerners. But that had all now come to an end.

CHAPTER FOURTEEN

Within weeks of arriving back in Cairns, I had made the decision to leave. I felt I needed to be living in Brisbane, where I would have the companionship and support of other couples who had adopted children from Romania.

The financial security I had as a married woman no longer meant anything to me. I felt I would rather spend the rest of my life living in poverty than in a soul-destroying relationship. Romania had done that to me. In Romania, I had decided not what I wanted to be in life, but what I wanted to become. I wanted to become true to myself. I already spent all week by myself, while my husband was out at the mine. In our fourteen years of marriage, he had not been at home much. For him, it was as if my trip to Romania had never happened, and he never talked about it. There was no talking of precious memories shared together.

I put the house on the market, and despite sale conditions

being very weak, it soon sold for a good price. I faxed the contracts, via a solicitor, to my husband at work. We had a telephone conference, and whilst I waited nervously, saying nothing, the solicitor patiently took the full force of Tony's anger, but he persisted in getting him to sign the contract of sale. I was free to go. There was nothing keeping me there.

A few days later, while I was on the phone, I happened to look across the road and saw a removal truck outside a neighbour's house; they were moving as well. I got the number of the removalists and rang their head office. The truck was returning to Brisbane and would take a back-load of furniture. The removalists came that afternoon and took a meagre amount of basic furniture to enable me to set up home in Brisbane with my girls.

I booked a flight to Brisbane for myself and the girls but had to cancel, as I was too nervous and sick with apprehension to leave on my own. A few days later I rebooked the flight and found the strength to follow through on my plans. I loaded the car with our things and put the car on a truck. Once in Brisbane, I found rental accommodation, enrolled Melannie in school for the start of a new year and established a healthy routine for myself and the girls.

The relief at ending an emotionally destructive 14-year marriage was enormous, far greater than I had expected. I had the usual struggles through the courts and the Child Support Agency for the property settlement and maintenance, but never wavered in my belief that I was entitled to my share and the maintenance. After six months of renting, I bought a two-bedroom ground floor unit with a fully-fenced courtyard. It was our little corner of the world. Melannie embarked on a very busy social life and continued to show a keen interest in all things fashionable.

One evening, after settling the girls in bed, we were in our new home, our little unit. Melannie had the smaller bedroom to herself and Natasha's cot was in my bedroom, the larger of the two. I went outside to clean the courtyard tiles with a long-handled brush. The tiles were filthy black and beer bottles were lying around. The property had previously been tenanted and was very neglected. As I started to scrub away, I felt a familiar pain in the right side of my abdomen. It began to get worse.

Scared now, I put down the brush and went inside and stood over Natasha, about eighteen months old now, sleeping peacefully in her cot. I could no longer ignore the pain, which had plagued me regularly during the last year. So back I went to see dear old Dr Monks, who was soon to retire. He simply said to me, "If my wife were in that much pain, I would operate."

Fortunately, I was not yet divorced and I was still covered under my husband's insurance policy, part of his employment package. I arranged for Tony to come down to Brisbane from Cairns to look after the girls while I went in for surgery.

In the operating theatre, I lay in pain on the hard, narrow surface of the operating table and screamed, "Don't take my baby, don't take my baby!" The words echoed loudly around the walls of the theatre, but the two nurses who remained to clean up took no notice and continued with their duties. Dr Monks and the other surgeon assisting him, who had both spent one and a half hours operating on me, had already left.

Thankfully, I drifted back to sleep, to wake up again in a ward. The ward was next to the office and I could hear the charge nurse doing the handover to the staff on afternoon shift. I heard her say that I had had my appendix out, as well as my remaining ovary, and extensive amounts of adhesions removed.

When Dr Monks arrived some time later to check on my progress, I joked with him, "Did you take out my appendix to save me coming back later?" By now I had had six operations.

"No," he replied. "Your appendix was very badly inflamed."

"How long had it been like that?"

"A year."

I had been unwell during the previous year, but I had kept going as I was busy with moving and all that entailed, and looking after my two beautiful girls.

But within hours of arriving home from the hospital, only a few days after the surgery, I started to vomit. We called Dr Monks, who advised that I should return urgently to hospital. I should have gone by ambulance. Instead, my ex-husband drove me across the city to the hospital with the girls sitting in the back seat. I was in a very distressed state by the time I arrived. A nurse met us at the car with a wheelchair.

A few more days recovering from major surgery was what I needed before being discharged once again. My ex-husband stayed on to help for approximately another four days, but after that he returned to work and I was left on my own.

I probably should not have been driving, but Melannie needed to get to school and grocery shopping and errands needed to be attended to.

A visit to my solicitor made me aware that as a single mother with two dependent children, I was entitled to more money from the property settlement than I had previously been led to believe. It wasn't a large amount, but I had to battle my ex-husband for it. I had no job and all the bills. He had a good job and no bills.

The additional money was enough to secure a mortgage on a house with a granny flat. No easy task as a single mother. Thankfully, an elderly bank manager gave me a loan, saying 'The rent on the granny flat will pay the mortgage'.

So, after a year in our little unit, I sold it and we moved to the house with the granny flat in a family friendly suburb. The house served its purposes for nine years, until it was time to move again, this time to a unit in an inner-city suburb, as that was all I could afford. It was within walking distance of the Catholic Primary School and High School which Natasha attended and closer to the city for University for Melannie, where she completed a degree in Business Management, majoring in Public Relations.

My father had lots of favourite sayings. "If you don't stop crying I will give you something to cry about" was one of them. Those were the words I remember him saying when I was growing up. 'You made your bed, you lie in it' was another of his sayings. After I left home there was the occasional letter from him from New Zealand and the occasional postal note with $80 in it at Christmas time and rarely, a phone call. I sent a few photos with letters and tried to maintain contact by phoning. Unfortunately, I always rang at the wrong time; he was either too tired or listening to the news, or it was dinner time. Conversations were extremely brief.

He had worked hard all his life to support his large family and himself and was extremely frugal. He was very proud of the home he had bought in Dunedin, where he lived independently for over thirty years until he was ninety-two.

One morning, there was an urgent phone-call from a brother in New Zealand whom I hadn't spoken to for a very long time.

'You're still my sister,' he said, and proceeded to inform me that our father had sustained a serious head injury after a fall in his beloved garden, and had been taken to hospital. From there he went to a nursing home. He had been there for the last few weeks, and wasn't expected to live.

I phoned the nursing home and had a conversation with him, brief as usual. He had a beautiful view outside the big bay windows of his bedroom and the home was newly built. From his window, he could see the seagulls sitting on the power-lines overhead.

I had one other brief conversation with him before he died. With his passing, my father gave me something to cry about, just as he had said he would all those years ago. There was a live feed of his funeral, so I was able to watch on my computer, with a girlfriend sitting next to me.

Tragically, a few months later there was another death in the family with my ex-husband committing suicide.

Article from Adoption Today Magazine, July 2016 issue: 'Building My Adoption Support Team'

Within a year of adopting Natasha, my husband was living elsewhere and I was a single mother to two beautiful girls. This was the inevitable result of a very dysfunctional marriage, one in which I did not have the support of my husband in adopting, apart from filling in boxes in the necessary paperwork and allowing me to have some money.

I had travelled alone to Romania, via Germany, and back home again via Germany and New Zealand, where I needed to finalise the adoption as a New Zealand citizen. My ex-husband didn't finally meet his adopted Romanian daughter until I returned home, two months after I had left.

I implore you, if you are reading this and married, make sure you travel together and support each other on your adoption journey. Meeting your adopted child for the first time in their country of origin is an essential part of the initial and ongoing bonding process as parents. So much so that government authorities now recognise this and make it an essential criterion that adopting couples travel together and stay in the child's country of origin for several weeks at least.

Feeling isolated and with no support where I was living in Cairns, I sold our house, packed up what remained of our belongings after a garage sale, and moved to Brisbane

with my two daughters. Natasha had just turned one and Melannie had just turned seven. We spent the first week living with my eldest brother, Stuart, his wife Ruth, and their two children, prior to moving into a house which I rented.

Now in Brisbane, I actively went about building my adoption support team. The International Adoptive Families of Queensland association, of whom

Deborah-Lee Furness was a patron, was an essential part of my adoption support team. I was already a member of IAFQ, having joined the organisation at the beginning of the three-and-a-half-year period which it took to become approved to adopt from overseas by the relevant government departments. During that time, I spoke with other members over the phone and looked forward to receiving their regular newsletters, which were a vital link, but I had never met anyone in person.

Having had this previous contact made the next step of attending 'chat and plays' much easier. Chat and plays were held in the homes of other members, or in local parks and gardens, of which Brisbane boasts many beautiful ones.

It wasn't long before I was asked to take on a more active role. I was asked to co-ordinate the first seminar on Inter-

Country Adoption and subsequently co-ordinated two more. Co-ordinating the seminars provided me with an opportunity to be more actively involved in the adoption community. It boosted my confidence and I thought it would look good on a resume as a single mother job-seeker. Although I was a fully qualified general and maternity trained nurse, I was unable to pursue this career path, as it meant six months of updating my training and shift work, but I had no one to look after my girls whilst I did shift work or during school holidays etc.

Janet, whom I had first met at the Gara De Nord railway station in Bucharest, and her husband were from Brisbane. They were originally from New Zealand and adopted a baby boy and a baby girl. When I first arrived in Brisbane, Janet was one of the first people I contacted.

Another couple I had met in Bucharest were Tina and Steve, also originally from Brisbane, who were adopting a baby boy and a toddler, a little girl. They arrived back in Brisbane after spending a year in their original home country of England, where they finalised their adoption.

Narelle, married to a New Zealand man and wanting to adopt, made enquiries and learnt that they could adopt from Romania as New Zealand citizens. Narelle and her husband were the first couple in Australia to adopt from Romania. They went to the media with their story after adopting a baby boy and a baby girl. Her story was the catalyst for mine and other adoptions at a time when the Australian government had banned adoptions from Romania, whereas the New Zealand government, in conjunction with Intercountry Adoption New Zealand, were facilitating these adoptions and assisting parents with the legal requirements established by both the New Zealand and Romanian authorities.

Tina had a suitable home with a downstairs rumpus room

and a big backyard with a sandpit and fort-style cubby house for the children to play in. It wasn't long before Tina, Narelle and I were meeting on a Thursday morning for playgroup. Tina always made egg sandwiches for a morning tea of food we brought to share. Our children are young adults now, but we still meet regularly and stay in contact.

From the age of eleven, my youngest sister, Alena and I were babysitting our neighbours' two young girls. After my mother died when I was thirteen, I helped parent my youngest brother, Kent, who was barely six years old at the time.

I was already interested in parenting issues when, during my nursing training, lectures on John Bowlby's pioneering work on maternal deprivation caught my attention. His research subsequently became known as 'Attachment Theory'. Armed with this knowledge, I went to Romania with the understanding that it would be better to adopt a baby under six months of age. On my return, I started reading all the research regarding the adverse effects of institutionalisation on Romania's abandoned children. My adoption support team, therefore, also included these academics, whose research helped me to understand why the adopted Romanian children were experiencing emotional and behaviour-related problems.

My website www.thepromisekept.co has several articles about the effects of institutionalisation on Romania's abandoned children.

The Hague Convention

The Hague Convention on Protection of Children and Co-operation in Respect of Inter-Country Adoption sets out the international principles which govern intercountry adoption. This multi-lateral treaty, approved by 66 countries on May

29th 1993 at The Hague, is designed to protect all parties involved in international adoption. The Convention seeks to protect vulnerable children from impoverished, intact families and orphanages from being abducted, bought and sold for the purpose of Human trafficking under the guise of an international adoption.

The Hague Convention entered into force in Australia in December 1998. It is implemented in the Family Law Act, 1975. New Zealand signed The Hague Convention in 1997. The Hague Convention entered into force in Australia in December 1998 and is implemented in the Family Law Act.

Romania ratified the United Nations Convention on the Rights of the Child in September 1990. (Law 18/1990). Romanian Law 11/1990 facilitated international adoptions. Romania ratified the Hague Convention on Protection of Children and Co-operation in Respect of Intercountry Adoption in 1994. (Law 84/1994).

International adoptions from Romania are rare. Adoption applicants must be at least eighteen years older than the child whom they are adopting. Both married couples and single women may apply to adopt from Romania, but at least one applicant must be a Romanian citizen. Children available for adoption will be three years or older and it can take up to three years to finalise an adoption.

Romania currently (2020) has approximately 50,400 abandoned children. 15,572 are in Foster care centres, 18,043 in foster families and 16,786 in family foster care. Only 3,274 are eligible for adoption: 1,139 for National Adoption and 2,135 for International Adoption.

Statistics from: Associatia Catharsis Brasov, a registered adoption agency and disability service. www.catharsis.org.ro

Since 2004, international adoptions have become virtually impossible, whereas domestic adoptions remain stable with approximately one thousand per year.

Source: Taylor and Francis On-line Adoption Quarterly Journal Volume 23, 2020.

For more information, please visit Associatia Catharsis Brasov, a Registered Adoption Agency, and Disability Support Service; www.catharsis.org.ro

Romania Without Orphans Alliance (Alianta Romania Fara Orfani), www.romaniafaraorfani.ro

In New Zealand, a small group of prospective adoptive parents formed a non-profit organisation, spearheaded by a Christian couple, Andrew and Sally Gardyne, and called it Inter-Country Adoption New Zealand, (I-CANZ). One of the founding members of this Inter-country Adoption support group, which lobbied politicians to allow adoptions from Romania, was Jonquil Graham. Jonquil has written three memoirs. Her book ''How Many Planes to Get Me'' tells the story of nine children adopted from Romania and Russia and the numerous children she and her husband, Bryan, have fostered. More recently, Jonquil has penned another memoir, ''Are All those Kids Yours? Fostering, Adoption, Teenagers.

Jonquil opened her heart and her home to many children of different nationalities. As I read her memoirs, I went on an emotional journey, laughing and crying. Laughing at her sense of humour, crying at her tragedies. Her books will encourage and inspire you, just as she has encouraged and inspired so many people she has encountered throughout her life's journey. Those of us who adopted from Romania as New Zealand citizens are indebted to people like Jonquil, Andrew and Sally for their tireless work in Inter-country Adoption reform.

Jonquil also wrote, "Once I was a Teenager"; Growing up in the 50s and 60s in Australia and Beyond.

Alex Kuch, a Romanian adoptee who was adopted in Germany and then moved with his family to New Zealand, was only eighteen when he first went to Romania and addressed Parliament asking for the re-opening of International Adoptions from Romania. Alex, a Public Figure, International Speaker, Orphan- advocate and New Zealand Ambassador for "I'm Adopted", is a graduate of Auckland University with a Bachelor of Arts degree in Politics and a Minor in Sociology.

Why is international adoption viewed so negatively? Perhaps it's because of the narrative that exists that says to take a child out of his or her country of origin would rob them of their culture. Alex explores this narrative in the following post; Current Concepts of Identity Outdated. Which can be found on the website; www.thepromisekept.co

POSTSCRIPT

Hardly a day goes by when I don't ask myself what would have become of Natasha, lying all day, unattended in a cot in urine-soaked clothing. International adoption has given her a future, the future that I promised her birth mother I would give her. I am immensely proud of what Natasha has accomplished.